Across America:
The Lewis and Clark Expedition
Revised Edition

DISCOVERY & EXPLORATION

DISCOVERY & EXPLORATION

Across America: The Lewis and Clark Expedition

Revised Edition

MAURICE ISSERMAN

JOHN S. BOWMAN and MAURICE ISSERMAN
General Editors

CHELSEA HOUSE
PUBLISHERS
An imprint of Infobase Publishing

Across America: The Lewis and Clark Expedition

Copyright ©2010 by Infobase Publishing

Chelsea House
An imprint of Infobase Publishing
132 West 31st Street
New York NY 10001

Library of Congress Cataloging-in-Publication Data
Isserman, Maurice.
  Across America : the Lewis and Clark expedition / by Maurice Isserman, John S. Bowman. — Rev. ed.
      p. cm. — (Discovery and exploration)
  Includes bibliographical references and index.
  ISBN 978-1-60413-192-5 (hardcover)
   1. Lewis and Clark Expedition (1804-1806)—Juvenile literature. 2. West (U.S.)— Discovery and exploration—Juvenile literature. 3. West (U.S.)—Description and travel—Juvenile literature. I. Bowman, John Stewart, 1931– II. Title. III. Series.
  F592.7.I87 2010
  917.804'2—dc22   2009018848

Chelsea House books are available at special discounts when purchased in bulk quantities for businesses, associations, institutions, or sales promotions. Please call our Special Sales Department in New York at (212) 967-8800 or (800) 322-8755.

You can find Chelsea House on the World Wide Web at
http://www.chelseahouse.com

Text design by Erika K. Arroyo
Cover design by Keith Trego

Printed in the United States of America

Bang FOF 10 9 8 7 6 5 4 3 2 1

This book is printed on acid-free paper.

All links and Web addresses were checked and verified to be correct at the time of publication. Because of the dynamic nature of the Web, some addresses and links may have changed since publication and may no longer be valid.

Contents

1

Monticello and Lemhi Pass
August 12, 1805

THE PRESIDENT OF THE UNITED STATES, THOMAS JEFFERSON, WAS spending the summer of 1805 at Monticello, his stately hilltop home in Virginia's Piedmont region. There, amid the tranquil beauties of his plantation's flower and herb gardens, he was able to escape for a while the pressures of office, as well as the heat, humidity, dust, and disease that the summer months brought to the nation's new capital in Washington, D.C. So Jefferson was not at the White House on Monday, August 12, 1805, when a long-expected wagonload of wooden boxes, trunks, and cages arrived there for him.

The shipment included animal skins, skeletons, antlers and horns, minerals, seeds, dried plants, a tin box containing insects and mice, a buffalo robe painted with the scene of a battle fought by American Indian tribes, an Indian bow and quiver of arrows, a live magpie, and something described on the list accompanying the shipment as a "living burrowing squirrel of the praries" (better known today as a prairie dog). This odd assortment had been packaged and sent to Jefferson four months earlier by his young friend and former aide, U.S. Army Captain Meriwether Lewis.

President Jefferson did not have a chance to examine the contents of Lewis's shipment for several months, but he was delighted to hear of their arrival. He instructed his servants at the White House to make sure that the skins and furs were well preserved and that the magpie and prairie dog were looked after (they were still alive when he got back to Washington in October). He also looked forward to the day when he

Meriwether Lewis left active military duty to serve as an aide to President Jefferson. His acute awareness and attention to detail were an asset to the president. They proved useful again in Lewis's journal entries and drawings.

would be able to hear firsthand from Captain Lewis about his adventures, but he knew it would be many months, perhaps even a year, before that would be possible. Meriwether Lewis and the small party of explorers that he led were at that moment somewhere deep in the American western wilderness, traversing a blank place on the existing maps of the North American continent, where non-Indian Americans had never before ventured.

SEARCH FOR THE NORTHWEST PASSAGE

The tale of Lewis and Clark begins long before they were born, in the time of Christopher Columbus. In 1492, the New World that Columbus encountered represented both an opportunity and an obstacle. Columbus had been searching for an old, not a new, continent. He had hoped to find a passage to the riches of Asia, an ocean crossing to replace the long, difficult land route. Instead, he stumbled upon the Americas—two continents previously unknown to Europeans, home to tens of millions of native peoples whose civilizations would in time be swept aside by the conquering powers from across the Atlantic. For the next three centuries after Columbus's landing in the New World, generation after generation of European explorers sought that elusive water route across the Americas.

In the course of the sixteenth century, Spanish and Portuguese explorers were able to establish that neither South nor Central America offered such a route. That left North America. Unlike the regions to the south that had been claimed by Spain and Portugal, the interior regions of North America and its western coastline remained largely unexplored and unsettled by Europeans and their American descendants century after century. The enticing possibility of finding a "Northwest Passage" through the Arctic regions of the North American continent or through some combination of rivers, lakes, and inland seas in the interior of the continent, excited the imagination of European explorers in the sixteenth and seventeenth centuries. They never found the opening to the Pacific that they sought so diligently, but the discoveries they made in the course of their search for the Northwest Passage helped lay the groundwork for the great rival North American empires of Great Britain and France.

THE MISSOURI: KEY TO THE NORTHWEST PASSAGE?

In 1673, French-Canadian explorer Louis Joliet and Jesuit missionary Jacques Marquette, accompanied by five voyageurs (boatmen skilled in wilderness travel), sailed from Canada down the Mississippi River as far south as present-day Arkansas. They came upon the mouth of a large river that emptied into the Mississippi, a river previously unknown to Europeans. This river, eventually named the Missouri after a local tribe, proved to be the principal tributary of the Mississippi.

THOMAS JEFFERSON'S SEARCH FOR AN EXPLORER

Jefferson is best remembered for his political achievements, but he once declared that the "tranquil pursuits of science" were his "supreme delight." He sought to increase his own knowledge and the knowledge of his countrymen in fields including agriculture, astronomy, cartography, geography, mathematics, meteorology, and natural history. Whenever he could—whenever political duties permitted—he devoted himself to his far-ranging scientific interests. Among the most compelling of those interests was the search for the Northwest Passage. It was not a task he could undertake himself; he was not a frontiersman and would, in fact, never venture farther west than Harper's Ferry, Virginia (later West Virginia). But he intended to do all he could to encourage others to take up the search. Late in 1783 Jefferson wrote to his friend and fellow Virginian, revolutionary war hero George Rogers Clark, asking if he would be interested in leading an expedition westward to explore the region "from the Mississippi to California." Jefferson was worried that if the Americans did not undertake the exploration of the unknown western half of the continent, the British would, in order to further their ambitions of "colonising into that quarter," as he put it. Clark found the prospect to be "Extreamly agreable," but had to decline Jefferson's offer. His service in the Revolutionary War had left his finances in disarray, and he could not take the time away from family responsibilities to lead a risky venture such as Jefferson proposed.

Soon afterward, Jefferson sailed to France where he served for five years as ambassador to the United States's most important European

THOMAS JEFFERSON'S OTHER EXPLORERS

Lewis and Clark's lasting fame, although certainly justified, has obscured the efforts of the other explorers who headed west in the years of Thomas Jefferson's presidency. Jefferson saw the Lewis and Clark expedition as just one part of an effort to learn more about the vast region of western North America. When Jefferson reported in February 1806 on Lewis and Clark's progress up the Missouri (based on information the two expedition leaders had sent back to Washington from their first winter encampment in North Dakota), he did so in a document entitled "Message from the President of the United States Communicating Discoveries Made in Exploring the Missouri, Red River, and Washita, by Captains Lewis and Clarke, Doctor Sibley, and Mr. Dunbar."

At Jefferson's request, William Dunbar, a Mississippi planter, and George Hunter, a Philadelphia chemist, led an expedition up the Ouchita River through northern Louisiana into present-day Arkansas in fall 1804. In spring 1805, a second Jefferson expedition set off up the Red River, this one led by Thomas Freeman, a civil engineer and surveyor, and Thomas Custis, a medical student. Dr. John Sibley joined them en route. Their 40-man expedition pushed up the Red River into present-day Texas, then part of the Spanish empire in the New World. On July 29, Spanish troops intercepted the American ally. But he did not stop thinking of the Northwest Passage. In 1785, Jefferson was in Paris when he met John Ledyard, a native of Connecticut who had been a member of British captain James Cook's famous third expedition exploring the Pacific. Ledyard's speculations about the lucrative possibilities of establishing a Pacific trade route, where sea otter furs gathered in the Pacific Northwest could be traded in China for luxury goods, greatly interested Jefferson, and he was pleased when the explorer sought him out in Paris in 1785. He listened sympathetically while Ledyard described an ambitious plan to find the Northwest Passage.

Ledyard's plan had an interesting twist. Rather than making his way westward up the Missouri, Ledyard proposed tackling the problem

explorers at a spot on the Red River known ever since as Spanish Bluff, about 30 miles (48 kilometers) northwest of present-day Texarkana, Texas. The Spanish commander bluntly told them that they had to return to where they came from or be taken into custody.

After Lewis and Clark, the best-known explorer of Jefferson's era was undoubtedly another army officer, Lieutenant Zebulon Montgomery Pike. Pike was born in Lamberton, New Jersey, in 1779, the son of an American military officer. Following his father's example, Pike joined the U.S. Army at the age of 15, and he served on the Ohio frontier in the 1790s. In July 1806, Pike led an expeditionary party west from St. Louis, up the Missouri River, then along the Arkansas River, and finally, on horseback, crossing the Kansas plains into Colorado. There they were the first Americans to encounter the Front Range of the Colorado Rockies. (One of those peaks has since been known as Pike's Peak.) Like the Freeman expedition, Pike's party ran into Spanish troops, who put them under arrest for trespassing onto Spanish lands. Pike and some of his men were released to U.S. authorities in Louisiana on June 30, 1807. Other members of the party were later released. "Language cannot express the gaiety of my heart when I once beheld the standards of my country waved aloft," Pike said of his return.

from another direction altogether. He would set out heading eastward from Europe, crossing Russia by land, sailing across the Pacific on a Russian trading vessel to the west coast of North America, and then, somehow, alone and on foot, find his way eastward across the Continental Divide to the Missouri River and eventually all the way to the Mississippi. It was a harebrained scheme, but Jefferson was sufficiently intrigued. Little came of the plan. Ledyard set out across Russia in 1788 but was arrested by the Russian authorities before he was halfway across the country and was forced to return to Europe.

In 1792, André Michaux, a French botanist living in the United States, came up with a proposal to lead an expedition to find the Northwest Passage. Before Michaux could set out up the Missouri, he got mixed up in a shady international conspiracy to reestablish French influence in the Louisiana Territory. The dream of finding the Northwest Passage had run into another dead end. But before the project fell through, an 18-year old U.S. Army officer named Meriwether Lewis had written to Jefferson asking if he could be a member of the expedition. Jefferson, who knew Lewis and his family from Virginia, kept his name in mind for future service.

THE DISCOVERY OF THE COLUMBIA RIVER

For nearly 30 years, there had been speculation in America and Britain about the existence of a river variously called the "Ouragon," the "Oregan," or the "Oregon," emptying into the Pacific somewhere north of California, with its headwaters in the Rocky Mountains somewhere near those of the Missouri. Robert Rogers, the commander of Roger's Rangers during the French and Indian War, had tried unsuccessfully after the war to interest the British government in sponsoring him on an expedition to discover this river. The existence of an Oregon River was pure hypothesis on the part of explorers and geographers because no white man had ever actually seen, let alone sailed upon it. Captain Cook's exploration of the Pacific coast had turned up no evidence of its existence.

Where the explorers failed, a private businessman succeeded. In the late eighteenth century an increasing number of merchant ships were prowling the coast of the Pacific Northwest, trading rum, muskets, beads, and other manufactured goods to the coastal tribes in exchange for furs, especially the highly valued fur of the sea otters found in those waters. As John Ledyard had predicted, there were fortunes to be made carrying the sea otter furs to Chinese ports, where they could be traded for spices, silks, and other luxury goods, which could then be sold for huge profits in London or Boston. In 1792, an American sea captain named Robert Gray, sailing out of Boston to the Pacific Northwest on just such a fur-trading voyage, discovered the mouth of a great river emptying into the Pacific. The Oregon River really did exist, and the dream of finding a northwest passage now seemed closer than ever to being realized.

Gray, however, did not call the river by the name Oregon. Instead he named it the Columbia River, after his ship the *Columbia Redivivia*. The discovery of the Columbia by an American gave the United States a somewhat questionable claim to the Oregon Territory. The Stars and Stripes was the first national flag to fly over the Columbia estuary. But Gray was just a private sailor in a merchant ship, acting without any official connection to the U.S. government. Moreover, he generously shared information about the location of the Columbia's mouth with a Royal Navy captain named George Vancouver who was on a mission of exploration in the same region. Vancouver's subordinate, Lieutenant William Broughton, and his men sailed 100 miles (160.9 kilometers) inland, much farther than Gray had gone. At a point of land just past the site of present-day Portland, Oregon, Broughton stepped ashore and declared the surrounding lands to be the possession of the British Crown. Broughton also named some of the most prominent geographical features visible from the river, including two of the snow-capped volcanoes of the Cascades range, Mount Hood and Mount St. Helens.

With the long-standing Spanish claim to California, and the new British claim to the Oregon Territory, the entire Pacific coast of the North American continent seemed likely to end up as the permanent possession of European colonial powers. Taken together, Spanish and British control of much of the Pacific coast (along with Russian control of Alaska) might shut U.S. traders out of the increasingly lucrative trade in furs with the coastal American Indians. If there were such a thing as a northwest passage, its western terminus would be in the hands of a foreign power. At the end of the eighteenth century, it thus seemed unlikely that the infant republic of the United States, whose westernmost territory then came to an end on the eastern bank of the Mississippi River, would ever become the nation whose lands extended "from sea to shining sea."

PRESIDENT JEFFERSON FINDS HIS EXPLORER

Shortly before his inauguration as third president of the United States in the late winter of 1801, Thomas Jefferson wrote a letter to Meriwether Lewis, the man who eight years earlier had volunteered to go along on the ill-fated expedition with André Michaux. Lewis was now 26 years old and a captain in the U.S. Army. "Dear Sir," Jefferson wrote, "The appointment to the Presidency of the U.S. has rendered it necessary for me to have a private secretary." He thought the young army officer would prove the ideal man for the job, even though Lewis had never been to Washington, D.C., or served in any administrative post in the government. While helping Jefferson with his official correspondence and other matters, Lewis could retain his rank as a captain in the U.S. Army. "Dear Sir," Lewis wrote in reply to the president on March 10, "I most cordially acquiesce, and with pleasure accept the office . . ."

Born on August 18, 1774, on a plantation called Locust Hill in Albermarle County, Virginia (not far from Monticello), he was the son of William Lewis and Lucy Meriwether Lewis. The Lewis family found its fortunes dramatically changed by the American Revolution, which broke out when Meriwether was a toddler. Shortly after he turned five years old in 1779, his father, a lieutenant in the Continental army, died while returning to the war from a leave to visit his family. Meriwether Lewis did not grow up with any fondness for the British or their colonial ambitions in North America.

Lewis learned the skills necessary for a Virginia planter: riding, overseeing slaves, and keeping account books. His mother was noted for her skills in herbal medicine, and she may have given him an eye for plants and their uses, which would later prove extremely useful. In 1795, he enlisted in the Virginia militia and marched off to the frontier to help put down a backwoods rebellion sparked by frontiersmen who resented paying federal taxes (known as the Whiskey Rebellion). It was not much of a rebellion, and all the excitement was over before Lewis got there. But he found that he liked the soldier's life, and transferred to the U.S. Army.

In 1801, Lewis was serving as paymaster for the U.S. Army's First Infantry Regiment, whose headquarters were in Pittsburgh. He was a capable officer but may well have wondered about his future; the military being so small and so inactive, there was not much scope for promotion. All things remaining equal, Lewis might have lived his life in obscurity, the command of a backwoods military outpost the greatest achievement of his life.

All that changed in March 1801 when the letter from Jefferson arrived. Within the week Lewis was en route to Washington, arriving at the start of April. For the next two years he lived as part of Jefferson's household in the official residence that was then called the President's House and would later be known as the White House. Lewis had a room on the second floor in the east wing of the building; Jefferson lived in the west wing. When Jefferson went home to Monticello for summer vacations, Lewis accompanied him. His tasks, for the most part, were routine. He conferred with Jefferson on military and political appointments, carried messages to Congress for the president, and wrote letters on official business. But the company could not have been better.

Sometime during those two years they spent in each other's company, most likely in summer or fall 1802, Jefferson decided that Lewis was the man to lead an American expedition up the Missouri. Although the young army officer was not trained as a scientist, Jefferson could see qualities in Lewis that were probably more important to the success of such a daring undertaking than a thorough scientific education. Jefferson believed that Lewis had a remarkable gift for "accurate observation" that would allow him to "readily single out whatever presents itself new to him" in the natural world, a habit of mind valuable to both the scientist and the explorer.

In December 1802, Jefferson asked the Spanish minister (or ambassador) in Washington, Carlos Martínez de Yrujo, if his government would have any objection if a small party of American explorers traveled up the Missouri River through the Louisiana Territory, an area controlled by Spain. He described it as a purely "literary" (meaning scientific) expedition. Martínez correctly suspected that the U.S. president was not being completely honest about the purposes of the proposed

This photograph shows the Missouri River in the present day. At 2,540 miles (4,090 km) in length, it is the longest river in North America. Lewis and Clark hoped that the river would lead them to the Northwest Passage.

mission. Jefferson, Martínez wrote to his superiors in Madrid, was "a lover of glory" as well as "a man of letters," and probably intended "to discover the way by which the Americans may some day extend their population and their influence up to the coasts of the South Sea [the Pacific]."

Jefferson ignored the unfriendly Spanish response. On January 18, 1803, he sent a confidential message to the U.S. Congress. "The river Missouri, & the Indians inhabiting it," the president declared, "are not as well known as is rendered desireable by their connection with the Mississippi, & consequently with us." Jefferson proposed a remedy for this problem:

> *An intelligent officer with ten or twelve chosen men, fit for the enterprize and willing to undertake it, from our posts, where they may be spared without inconvenience, might explore the*

whole line, even to the Western ocean, have conferences with the [American Indians] on the subject of commercial intercourse, get admission among them for our traders as others are admitted, agree on convenient deposits for an interchange of articles, and return with the information acquired in the course of two summers.

In his dealings with Congress, as with the Spanish ambassador, Jefferson was being less than completely honest. His emphasis on the benefits the expedition might yield for American merchants, although certainly a concern of Jefferson's, was not the main purpose of the expedition. He said nothing of the scientific observations that he hoped his "intelligent officer" would carry out en route—he rather doubted whether as president he had the authority under the Constitution to launch an expedition for that purpose. And the possibility that the expedition might find a route all the way to the "Western ocean," was mentioned almost as an afterthought. Any implications such a discovery might have for the expansion of American territory westward to the Pacific were left unspoken. In any case, candid or not, Jefferson's message to Congress produced the results he wished for. In February Congress authorized the expedition, with an appropriation for the sum he asked to pay for it (although the $2,500 that Congress appropriated turned out to be about one-sixteenth of the eventual cost).

2

Preparing the Way
March 1803 to May 1804

IN SPRING 1803, MERIWETHER LEWIS GRAPPLED WITH THE daunting question of determining what a dozen or more explorers need to bring with them when crossing thousands of miles of wilderness on river and by foot, across plains, through forests, and over mountains, exposed to summer's heat and winter's cold. Uncertain of the route and the reception they might receive from the native inhabitants, Lewis also had to consider what was needed for the group's protection.

Among the things Lewis and his men certainly were going to need were firearms, both to defend and feed themselves. So in mid-March, Lewis left Washington and traveled to the federal arsenal at Harpers Ferry, Virginia. No party traveling west of the Mississippi River had ever carried as impressive a set of weaponry as the rifles that Lewis acquired. Lewis ordered 15 of the .54 caliber Model 1803 short rifles, the first the arsenal had ever produced. They were easier to load and considerably more accurate than the then-standard infantry musket. He also acquired knives, tomahawks, and pistols.

He also had a special request for the skilled blacksmiths at the arsenal. He asked them to fabricate an iron frame for an experimental portable boat of Lewis's own design. The entire iron frame for the 30-foot (9 meter-)-long vessel could be broken down into 10 sections, each weighing about 22 pounds. If the expedition should come to a difficult portage, either along the Missouri or when it reached the Rockies, and was forced to abandon its boats, he believed that the frame could be lugged overland and down to the next navigable water, then reassembled and covered in animal skins. Lewis believed it would prove a river-worthy craft, capable of carrying up to 8,000 pounds in passengers and supplies. He did not, however, have time to test his theory before ordering the frame to be shipped westward.

In mid-April, Lewis rode on to Lancaster, Pennsylvania. There, Jefferson had arranged for him to be schooled in the art of making celestial observations by the eminent astronomer Andrew Ellicott, another of the president's associates in the American Philosophical Society, an organization of intellectuals. Ellicott's lessons would help Lewis plot his location by the position of the stars, establishing a record of longitude and latitude as he moved up the Missouri.

In the first week of May Lewis moved on to Philadelphia, where he would spend the next month. He divided his time between meetings with more of Jefferson's scientific friends and securing supplies for the expedition. Lewis would serve as the expedition's doctor as well as its commander, and his Philadelphia mentors included the most famous physician in America, Benjamin Rush. However, most of Rush's advice would prove less than useful where it was not actually harmful to the patients under Lewis's care. It was Rush's considered belief, for example, that powerful laxatives were the first line of defense against disease.

While in Philadelphia, Lewis stocked up on 600 doses of "bilious pills," or laxatives, for his medical kit. The herbal lore Lewis learned from his mother would, in the actual event, prove far more beneficial than the pills that the soldiers on the expedition would come to call "Rush's Thunderbolts." Rush also suggested that in the case of the "least indisposition" on the trail, the explorers should "not attempt to overcome it by labor or marching. Rest in a horizontal position." If that advice had been taken literally, it is doubtful that the expedition would have ever reached the Pacific.

Among the other supplies Lewis purchased in Philadelphia were scientific and navigational instruments, including a chronometer (an accurate clock set to Greenwich Mean Time, necessary for calculating longitude), iron goods, copper kettles, shirts, and fishing tackle. From Israel Wheelen, a Philadelphia merchant, he bought 80 "pocket Looking glasses," 72 pieces of striped silk ribbon, and 30-odd pounds of white, yellow, red, and blue beads, all intended as presents or for bartering with the Western Indians. By the time Lewis left Philadelphia, he had spent nearly all the money that he and Jefferson had told Congress would be necessary to pay for the entire expedition, and he had yet to purchase any of the boats he would need to carry his men up the Missouri River.

JEFFERSON'S ORDERS

By June 7, Lewis was back in Washington. Over the next few weeks, he and the president doubtless spent many hours together in the White House going over their plans. On June 20, Jefferson issued his final instructions for the expedition. "The object of your mission," Jefferson wrote to Lewis, "is to explore the Missouri river, & such principal stream of it, as by it's course and communication with the waters of the Pacific ocean, whether the Columbia, Oregan, Colorado or any other river may offer the most direct & practicable water communication across this continent for the purposes of commerce." Lewis was to keep careful notations of latitude and longitude of all distinguishing features of the Missouri and Columbia rivers and the landscape through which the great rivers passed, "especially at the mouths of rivers, at rapids, at islands, & other places & objects distinguished by such natural marks & characters of a durable kind, as that they may with certainty be recognised hereafter." And, most important, he was to employ his new skills in fixing longitude and latitude to determine the location of the "interesting points of the portage between the heads of the Missouri, & of the water offering the best communication with the Pacific ocean. . . ."

Jefferson insisted that Lewis take every possible precaution to ensure that the information he gathered be carefully recorded and preserved. "Several copies of these," Jefferson ordered in reference to Lewis's geographical records, "as well as of your other notes should be made at leisure times & put into the care of the most trustworthy of your attendants . . ." As for what those "other notes" should include, Jefferson specified that Lewis was to make note of the "names of the [Indian] nations & their numbers" he encountered en route, as well as observations of their relations with other tribes, their languages, their economy, their society, their culture, and their religions.

Jefferson made a long list of "other objects worthy of notice" for Lewis and the expedition, including animals, minerals, climate, and plants. Returning again to the necessity for guaranteeing that a copy of his notes survive, Jefferson urged Lewis to take advantage of any circumstances that would allow him to send back to Washington, perhaps by friendly American Indian couriers, or by any merchant ship they might encounter on the Pacific coast, "a copy of your journal, notes & observations of every kind. . . ." This was the only time Jefferson used the word *journal* in his instructions to Lewis, and then only in passing, but it is a word that will always be linked with the expedition. In carrying out President Jefferson's orders, Captain Lewis was required, not only to be an explorer and a military commander, but also a writer. And in this last endeavor, he proved to have gifts that even Jefferson, his intimate companion and great admirer, never suspected. The journals that Lewis kept over the next several years would prove his greatest single legacy to subsequent generations of Americans.

LEWIS FINDS A CO-COMMANDER

President Jefferson closed his list of instructions to Captain Lewis by reminding him of one final duty: "To provide, on the accident of your death, against anarchy, dispersion, & the consequent danger to your party, and total failure of the enterprize, you are hereby authorized . . . to name the person among them who shall succeed to command on your [death]. . . ."

Jefferson and Lewis had, in fact, already agreed on their candidate for second in command. Lewis had first met William Clark in 1795 at Fort Greenville, Ohio. There he served under Clark's command in an army rifle company for six months. Like Lewis, Clark was

William Clark came from a family of adventurous American frontiersmen. It took Clark only one day to accept Lewis's offer to join the expedition. He wrote to Lewis, "This is an undertaking fraited with many difficulties, but My Friend I do assure you that no man lives withe whome I would perfur to undertake Such a Trip &c. as your self. . ."

a Virginian by birth. He was born August 1, 1770, in Caroline County, Virginia, the ninth child in a family of 10 children. One of his older brothers was George Rogers Clark, a hero of frontier fighting during the American Revolution, and the man who Jefferson had first asked to lead an expedition in search of the Northwest Passage back in 1783.

When Clark was 14, his family moved to a plantation near the Falls of the Ohio in Indiana Territory, across the river from present-day Louisville, Kentucky. He joined the Kentucky militia in 1789 and transferred to the U.S. Army in 1792. Like Lewis, he was an accomplished woodsman, and he was an impressive commanding figure, more than six feet tall. Among his distinguishing features was his hair color; some of the American Indians who met him would call him the "Red-Headed Chief." Unlike Lewis, he had actually been involved in fighting the American Indians, including the decisive battle of Fallen Timbers in 1794 that secured the Ohio Valley for white settlement. Clark resigned his commission in the army in 1796 to look after family business. Lewis had occasional contact with Clark in the years that followed, but they had not been close personal friends.

"Dear Clark," Lewis wrote on June 19, 1803: "From the long and uninterupted friendship and confidence which has subsisted between us I feel no hesitation in making to you the following communication under the fulest impression it will be held by you inviolably secret . . ." Lewis described at some length the mission he had been given and ended with a personal plea to Clark: "If therefore there is anything under those circumstances, in this enterprise, which would induce you to participate with me in it's fatiegues, it's dangers and it's honors, believe me there is no man on earth with whom I should feel equal pleasure in sharing them as with yourself."

It took a month for Lewis's letter to reach Clark at his home in Kentucky, and it took him but a day to make up his mind. "Dear Lewis," he wrote on July 18, 1803: "I received by yesterdays Mail, your letter of the 19th . . . The Contents of which I received with much pleasure. . . . This is an undertaking fraited [freighted] with many dificulties, but My friend I do assure you that no man lives whith whome I would perfur to undertake Such a Trip &c. [etc.] as your self . . ." Lewis had assured Clark that although Lewis would be nominally in command, they would in fact function on the expedition as co-commanders, and that Clark could resume his former army rank of captain. What had started out as the Lewis expedition was now to be known to posterity as the Lewis and Clark Expedition.

THE LOUISIANA PURCHASE

When Jefferson had first discussed with Lewis the possibility of sending him up the Missouri in search of the Northwest Passage, both men had known that this involved a venture not only into the wilderness but into foreign territory. The moment that Lewis and his party of explorers left the east bank of the Mississippi to cross over to the mouth of the Missouri, they would be leaving U.S. soil. Added to the dangers of the wilderness, and of possibly hostile American Indian tribes, Lewis might well find himself challenged and detained by unfriendly Spanish authorities.

The Louisiana Territory, including the city of New Orleans at the mouth of the Mississippi River, had been ceded by France to Spain in 1762, near the end of the French and Indian War. The Spanish were pleased with the deal because they could use the Louisiana Territory as a buffer zone between their long-established colonies in Mexico and the Southwest, and the British colonies on the Atlantic Coast. Spain had been the center of Europe's most powerful empire in the sixteenth and seventeenth centuries. But by the late eighteenth century, its power was waning in Europe and in the New World. The Spanish flag flew over New Orleans and the little frontier outpost far upriver called St. Louis, but most of the European residents of the territory remained French-speaking. After the American Revolution, land-hungry American settlers were pouring into the Ohio and Mississippi valleys; some were crossing the Mississippi and entering Spanish-controlled territory. Given time, U.S. leaders expected, the Spanish would inevitably be pushed aside in the Louisiana Territory by the pressure of migrating American settlers.

Expectations that the United States would one day inherit the lands west of the Mississippi were badly shaken by events abroad in 1800–1801, when Spain agreed to a proposal from French emperor Napoleon Bonaparte to swap the Louisiana Territory for land he controlled in northern Italy. After a 40-year absence, it looked like France was coming back to North America.

Jefferson was determined to head off the transfer of New Orleans to France. American diplomat Robert Livingston was in Paris, trying to negotiate the purchase of New Orleans from Napoleon's government. Negotiations were not going well. Napoleon planned to send an army of thousands of French soldiers to New Orleans as soon as they finished suppressing a slave rebellion in the French-controlled island of Saint-Domingue (present-day Haiti and the Dominican Republic) in the Caribbean. But the French army on Saint-Domingue met a fateful setback, as they became decimated by yellow fever and by the attacks of the rebellious slaves. Napoleon suddenly decided that he had more pressing business beating the British in Europe. In spring 1803, he ordered his negotiators to offer the Americans not just New Orleans, but the entire region of the Missouri watershed that stretched from the Mississippi to the Rocky Mountains, known as the Louisiana Territory. For the bargain price of $15 million, the American negotiators in Paris added 565 million acres to the territory of the United States. The Louisiana Purchase brought into U.S. possession the territory that would over the course of the nineteenth century become the states of Louisiana, Arkansas, Missouri, Iowa, Minnesota, North Dakota, South Dakota, Nebraska, Kansas, Oklahoma, and Montana, as well as about half the future states of Wyoming and Colorado.

Lewis now had the welcome assurance that he would be traveling through U.S. territory until he crossed over the Rockies. On July 5, Lewis left Washington heading westward. It would be two years, five months, and 25 days before he would return to Washington, D.C., to report to President Jefferson.

FROM THE OHIO TO THE MISSISSIPPI

Lewis's first stop after departing Washington was Harpers Ferry, to check on the supplies he had ordered from the federal arsenal. He then

(opposite page) In 1803, the United States doubled in size due to the acquisition of territory that make up portions of 14 current U.S. states and 2 Canadian provinces. One of the largest land transactions in history, the Louisiana Territory was purchased for $15 million. Lewis and Clark were then sent by Thomas Jefferson to explore the territory of the Louisiana Purchase.

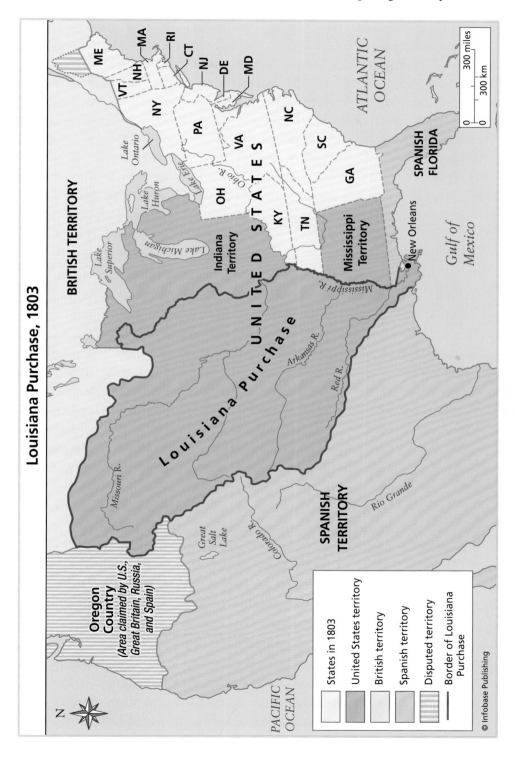

Louisiana Purchase, 1803

BRITISH TERRITORY

ATLANTIC OCEAN

ME
NH
MA
VT
RI
CT
NY
NJ
PA
DE
MD
NC
VA
SC
GA

U N I T E D   S T A T E S

OH
KY
TN

Lake Ontario
Lake Erie
Lake Huron
Lake Superior
Lake Michigan
Ohio R.

Indiana Territory

Mississippi Territory

SPANISH FLORIDA

New Orleans

Gulf of Mexico

Mississippi R.

L o u i s i a n a   P u r c h a s e

Arkansas R.
Red R.
Missouri R.

SPANISH TERRITORY

Rio Grande

Great Salt Lake
Colorado R.

Oregon Country
(Area claimed by U.S., Great Britain, Russia, and Spain)

PACIFIC OCEAN

N

States in 1803
United States territory
British territory
Spanish territory
Disputed territory
Border of Louisiana Purchase

300 miles
300 km

© Infobase Publishing

rode on to Pittsburgh, where he had contracted with a local boatbuilder to construct a large keelboat. One wagonload of supplies would follow him to Pittsburgh from Harpers Ferry; another was already en route from Philadelphia. Eight soldiers from the fort at Carlisle, Pennsylvania, would also join Lewis in Pittsburgh, to take the keelboat down the Ohio River. They would not accompany the expedition up the Missouri. Lewis was to recruit his expedition members from army posts they would pass while traveling en route to St. Louis.

Lewis looked forward to seeing the keelboat, which according to the assurances he had received from the builder, would be ready to launch by July 20. The craft was to be 55 feet long, 8 feet wide, with a 32-foot mast, a cabin in the stern, and capable of carrying 10 tons of supplies and a crew of two dozen. It could be propelled by its sails, by 22 oars, by poles, or by towropes, depending on conditions the expedition met along the Missouri. Lewis was in for a disappointment. The boatbuilder much preferred drink to work, and it would be nearly the end of August before the keelboat was completed. While he waited, he took delivery of the supplies from Harpers Ferry and Philadelphia, and he took command of seven of the eight soldiers who were supposed to accompany him down the Ohio (one deserted before reaching Pittsburgh). Clark's letter accepting his offer of co-command caught up with Lewis while he was in Pittsburgh, which came as welcome news. Lewis also recruited two volunteers, George Shannon and John Colter, who were to become part of the permanent expedition party.

Lewis had originally planned to reach St. Louis by the end of summer and to head up the Missouri some 200 or 300 miles (321 or 482 km) before making winter camp. But fall was coming on, and he still had 1,100 miles (1,770 km) to travel by river just to reach the mouth of the Missouri. Finally, on August 31, Lewis and his crew of 10 or possibly 11 men (the seven soldiers, two or possibly three new recruits, and a pilot who was to help them navigate the Falls of the Ohio) set off down the Ohio River. Seaman, a black Newfoundland dog that Lewis had bought for company in Pittsburgh for $20, accompanied them. There were now two boats in Lewis's little fleet: the keelboat and a pirogue that he also purchased in Pittsburgh (the *pirogue*, as Lewis used the term, was a flat-bottomed open boat that could be rowed or rigged with a sail).

Because of the shallow water in late summer, Lewis did not want to overload the boats. Some of the expedition supplies were sent overland by wagon to Wheeling, Virginia (now West Virginia), where the river deepened. Even with the lightened load, the men frequently had to get out, unload and portage the cargo downriver, and then drag the boats through shallow places in the river. They had other troubles as well, further slowing their progress. Rain was rusting their rifles, tomahawks, and knives and spoiling the supply of biscuits, forcing them to halt to dry their goods and repackage them. The pirogue Lewis acquired in Pittsburgh leaked, as did a replacement craft he picked up en route a few days later. In Wheeling, on September 9, Lewis purchased a larger pirogue that served them better. It is difficult to keep track of the expedition's boats, but somewhere along the way en route to the Mississippi that fall, Lewis seems to have acquired both the red and the white pirogue that would carry his men up the Missouri.

Lewis was already keeping his eyes open for interesting natural phenomena that he could report to Jefferson. On September 11, he saw something that astonished him: a large number of gray squirrels swimming "light on the water" across the Ohio River. Lewis's interests in the swimming squirrels as a naturalist soon gave way to another interest: satisfying his appetite. He sent Seaman, the Newfoundland dog, into the river to kill some of the squirrels and fetch them back to the boat.

He continued his progress down the Ohio. Stopping in Cincinnati on September 28, Lewis took some time off from the journey to explore a local site known for its fossil remains. Lewis may have decided the delay was worthwhile because he knew how much Jefferson was fascinated by the science of paleontology. He packed up a box of bones, including some that he thought were remains of wooly mammoths, and shipped them back to Washington (they were lost en route, to Jefferson's disappointment).

On October 14, a month and a half after setting off from Pittsburgh, Lewis and his men reached Clarksville, in Indiana Territory, where William Clark lived with his older and ailing brother George Rogers Clark. The expedition was now beginning to take shape. At Lewis's request, Clark had been busy lining up recruits, and he introduced Lewis to seven young volunteers from Kentucky: William Bratton, George Gibson, John Shields, Charles Floyd, Nathaniel Pryor, and brothers Reuben and Joseph Field. They were sworn into the army along with Shannon and Colter. By the standards of the U.S. military in the early nineteenth century, these men were to be well compensated for their service. To attract qualified recruits, Lewis secured double pay for the men on the expedition ($10 a month for enlisted men, instead of the standard $5), plus the promise of early discharge on their return, and a western land bounty of several hundred acres for each man who went along. One man who joined the expedition at Clarksville would not be paid anything at all, however: That was York, an African-American slave owned by William Clark. York was a powerful, heavyset man with "short curling hair" about Clark's age, who had been his companion since childhood.

On October 26, after spending two weeks resting and refitting in Clarksville, Lewis and Clark and their men set off down the Ohio, passing through present-day Illinois. On November 11, they reached Fort Massac, an old French fortification located on a commanding promontory above the Ohio that had been restored by Americans. There they added two new recruits to the expedition's roster, John Newman and Joseph Whitehouse, plus a civilian, George Drouillard (in their journal entries, the captains would refer to him as "Drewyer"). Drouillard brought valuable skills to the expedition, including his ability to interpret the sign language that allowed American Indians of many different tribes and spoken languages to communicate among themselves. He was also a first-rate hunter and trail finder. He would prove well worth the $25 a month he was paid for his services. Lewis immediately dispatched Drouillard on a mission to another army post, South West Point, Tennessee, to find eight soldiers who were waiting there to join the expedition. When they finally caught up with the expedition five weeks later, Lewis rejected four of the men as unfit for wilderness travel.

On November 20, they set off northward up the Mississippi, the river that the Algonquian Indians called "the Father of Waters." Including its tributaries, the Mississippi River drains the water from 40 percent of the continental United States. Although the Mississippi's course was well known by this point, Clark began to record the river's twists and turns, with compass bearings, perhaps practicing the record-keeping he would need to keep along the Missouri.

As they headed northward, they were traveling between separate countries: the Illinois Territory, part of the United States, formed the east bank of the river, while the Louisiana Territory, which was still officially governed by the Spanish and was not scheduled to be handed over to the United States until the following spring, lay to the west. After two days, they passed by a U.S. settlement on the Spanish side of the river where 15 American families were already established, operating as the advance guard of thousands who would soon be pouring into the territory. They also passed keelboats heading up the river with dry goods and whiskey to sell to American settlers on the Illinois side, and other keelboats heading down to New Orleans loaded with furs. They reached the U.S. Army military post Fort Kaskaskia on the Illinois side of the river, on November 28, where they added at least six more volunteers to the expedition's strength.

THE EXPEDITION'S FIRST WINTER

Winter was coming on, and they would soon need to make a permanent encampment for its duration. At Fort Kaskaskia, Lewis and Clark split up. Lewis borrowed a horse and rode north along the Illinois side of the river, arriving at the American settlement at Cahokia, across the river from St. Louis, on December 7. He crossed the river to the city the following day. In 1803, St. Louis was celebrating the fortieth year since its founding. It was still a very small community of about 1,000 residents huddled along the banks of the Missouri.

On December 8, Lewis met with the Spanish governor of the city, Colonel Carlos Dehault Delassus. Colonel Delassus was not overly welcoming. He had as yet received no official notification of the Louisiana Purchase, and he reminded Lewis that as an American he was still a guest on foreign territory. And he made it clear that Lewis could not begin his exploration of the Missouri that winter—a plan that the captains had already abandoned in any case.

Lewis received a friendlier reception from the city's wealthy fur-trading merchants, including Manuel Lisa and half-brothers Auguste and Pierre Chouteau. The merchants knew that their own economic futures were bound up now with the westward expansion of the United States, and they were eager to ingratiate themselves with the new rulers of the Louisiana Territory, as well as to sell the American captain the goods he would need to outfit his ever-expanding expeditionary force. They proved useful sources of information on both the geography and

LEWIS'S MAP COLLECTION

Lewis needed to know what to expect in his search for the Northwest Passage. He needed maps. He got one of them from Nicholas King, surveyor for the newly founded city of Washington, D.C. At the request of Albert Gallatin, secretary of the treasury, King prepared a map for Lewis, drawing on the best available knowledge of western geography. The King map gave a fairly accurate representation of the Mississippi River, of the first few hundred miles of the Missouri River, and the Pacific coast around the mouth of the Columbia River. But in between those points, what little detail was given was labeled "conjectural"—which meant it was anybody's guess as to what actually would be found.

Lewis also had a map that Aaron Arrowsmith, a British mapmaker, had published in 1802 and that was advertised as "Exhibiting All the New Discoveries in the Interior Parts of North America." Arrowsmith's map showed Alexander Mackenzie's discoveries in Canada, as well as details of the upper Missouri provided by Hudson's Bay Company fur traders. Like the King map, Arrowsmith depicted the Rocky Mountains as a single and not very impressive mountain range.

When they reached St. Louis, Lewis and Clark were also able to obtain copies of maps drawn by James Mackay and John Evans, who had explored the Missouri as far as villages of the Mandan Indians in the 1790s on behalf of a Spanish-chartered fur-trading company. Although neither Evans or Mackay had traveled west of the Mandan villages, their maps provided useful details about that region, such as the location of the mouth of the Yellowstone River, as well as the location of a great falls along the Missouri. Their maps also suggested that the Rockies might prove a more formidable barrier than the single-ridge line usually depicted.

the American Indians of the Missouri, at least along its first few hundred miles as it stretched westward from St. Louis. Antoine Soulard, a Frenchman employed by the Spanish governor as surveyor-general for Upper Louisiana, provided Lewis with a copy of a map he had drawn, showing in detail the course of the Missouri up to the Mandan villages, and offering a speculative depiction of what lay further west.

While Lewis was attending to business in St. Louis, Clark led the rest of the expedition up the river, past St. Louis to the mouth of the Wood River. Here they would make their winter camp, at a site directly across the Mississippi from the mouth of the Missouri. What is known of the winter at Camp Wood comes almost entirely from Clark's journal. Lewis's silence as a writer would last, with brief exceptions, until April 1805. Clark was now the principal day-to-day recorder of the expedition's fortunes and progress. He tended to be terse and matter-of-fact at first, providing few details beyond the orders he gave the men and the weather. Thus the entry for December 13 read, in its entirety:

> *fixed on a place to build huts Set the men to Clearing land & Cutting logs—a hard wind all day—flying Clouds, Sent to the neghbourhood, Some Indians pass.*

It snowed on December 15.

By December 22, Clark was recording that the Mississippi was "[C]overd with running Ice." Gradually, Clark's journal-keeping grew more inventive and interesting. In addition to the record of turkeys shot and fights between the men, Clark began to insert sketches in his notebook, including several of the keelboat and one of the white pirogue. When the men finished building the huts, Clark put them to work improving the keelboat.

After a long absence in St. Louis and Cahokia, Lewis briefly rejoined the expedition in February. Clark got a welcome chance to cross the river to St. Louis and enjoy a little of its social life. (Camp life had not agreed with Clark that winter; "I was unwell" was a recurring entry in Clark's journal throughout January and early February.) Lewis spent only a few days at Camp Wood. For most of February both captains were in St. Louis, leaving Sergeant John Ordway in command. The captains' prolonged absences did not help the camp's disciplinary problems. The men may have resented the fact that their officers were getting to spend the winter enjoying the comforts of St. Louis, while they were stuck out in the woods, in freezing temperatures, with nothing to look forward to beyond their evening ration of whiskey. At times it seemed as if mutiny threatened the success of the expedition. Reuben Field refused to take his turn at guard duty, and other soldiers loudly and belligerently took his side. John Shields and John Colter defied Ordway's orders and threatened to kill him. Lewis could be a strict disciplinarian, but he decided not to discharge the troublemakers (possibly because there were too many of them).

"WE PROCEEDED ON . . ."

On March 10, 1804, the Stars and Stripes was raised over St. Louis. Lewis was there as the official representative of the U.S. government for the ceremony that saw the Louisiana Territory handed over, first from Spain to France, and then from France to the United States. They were no longer on foreign soil when they stood on the west bank of the Mississippi. That was certainly good news. So was the arrival of spring shortly thereafter. Lewis and Clark planned to get an early start up the Missouri. Clark calculated that they would travel 1,500 miles (2,414 km) to reach the Mandan villages, the last well-described location on their maps. His calculations were only about 100 miles (160 km) short of the actual distance. He further calculated that it would be 1,550 miles (2,494 km) from the Mandan villages to the Pacific Ocean. There he erred significantly; his calculations were 1,000 (1,600 km) miles too short. Making 10 or 12 miles a day (16 or 19 km), Clark figured the expedition should be able to travel as far as the headwaters of the Missouri in the Rocky Mountains by September 1804, and then push on the following spring to reach the Pacific in summer 1805.

Departure was set for April 18. The expedition hired seven French boatmen, known as *engagés,* who had experience sailing up the Missouri as far as the Mandan villages. But in the end, they were delayed. Lewis needed more time to obtain last-minute supplies, and he also had to make complicated arrangements for Pierre Chouteau to lead a delegation of Osage Indians to Washington, D.C., to meet their new "great white father," Thomas Jefferson.

By the time everything was sorted out, necessary supplies gathered and packed in the expedition's three boats, it was mid-May. Meanwhile,

Clark had received disappointing news from Washington. Despite Lewis's promise that Clark would hold rank equal to his own, Jefferson had secured him a commission only as a lieutenant. Clark was angry,

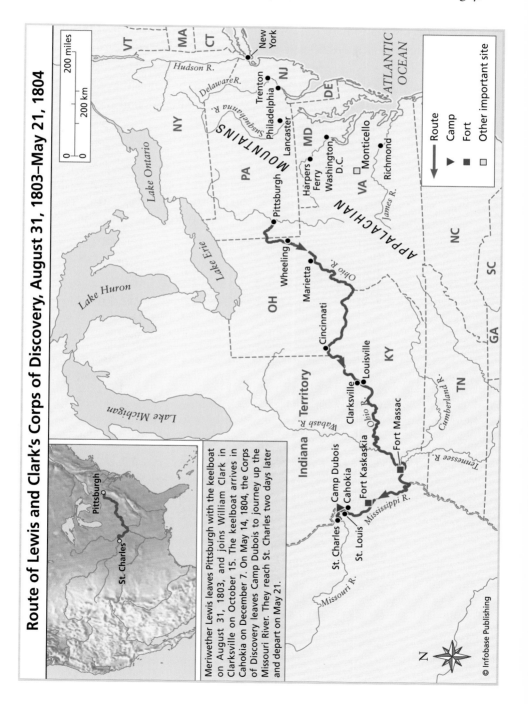

Route of Lewis and Clark's Corps of Discovery, August 31, 1803–May 21, 1804

Meriwether Lewis leaves Pittsburgh with the keelboat on August 31, 1803, and joins William Clark in Clarksville on October 15. The keelboat arrives in Cahokia on December 7. On May 14, 1804, the Corps of Discovery leaves Camp Dubois to journey up the Missouri River. They reach St. Charles two days later and depart on May 21.

© Infobase Publishing

and Lewis sympathized completely. The two officers agreed they would make no mention of the difference in rank to their men. Throughout the expedition Lewis referred to Clark as "Captain Clark," as most historians have done ever since.

Finally, on May 14, 1804, it was time to go. Lewis was in St. Louis, still tending to the Osage delegation. He would join the expedition after a few days. Clark was in command of the keelboat and the two pirogues. On the evening of May 14, he wrote in his journal: "I set out at 4 oClock P.M. in the presence of many neighboring inhabitents, and proceeded on under a jentle brease up the Missouri. . . ."

3

Up the Missouri
May to October 1804

LEWIS, CLARK, THE THREE SERGEANTS—ORDWAY, FLOYD, AND
Pryor (Clark's "4 Sergeants" seems to have been a slip of the pen)—along
with the 22 "Amns" (Americans), the three interpreters, and Clark's black
servant York constituted the expedition's permanent party. These were
the 31 men who were intended to go all the way to the Pacific and back.
They would travel on the keelboat. The "9 or 10 French" (a later list of
Clark's would account for only eight) were the engagés, the hired boatmen who would accompany the expedition only as far as the Mandan
villages. They traveled in the 41-foot-long (12-meters-long) red pirogue.
The remaining members, the "Corpl. and Six in a perogue," consisted of
Corporal Richard Warfington and his detachment (a later list by Clark
would account for only five men serving under Warfington) and were to
travel some distance up the Missouri with the permanent party but to
return before winter set in to St. Louis. They were assigned the smallest
vessel, the 35-foot-long (10.6-meters-long) white pirogue. Clark's somewhat undependable count of expedition members has led historians to
varying conclusions as to just how many men actually set sail on May 14,
with estimates ranging between 43 and 48.

LAST CONTACTS WITH
WHITE SETTLEMENTS

Departing in the late afternoon, the men of what Jefferson had dubbed
the "Corps of Discovery" made modest progress that first day. They
crossed the Mississippi and pushed a short way up the Missouri. They

camped that night by a small creek near Fort Belle Fontaine, in present-day North St. Louis. The men probably missed their snug cabins at Camp Wood, as it rained so steadily they could not keep their campfires burning. These first days of travel served as training for the men, as the experience gave them a more realistic taste of the upcoming adventure.

On May 16 they reached the little village of St. Charles, located on the north bank of the river, about 21 miles (33 km) upriver from the mouth of the Missouri. With its 450 inhabitants, St. Charles was the last substantial white settlement they would encounter until their return. Clark and the men spent five days there, waiting for Lewis to finish his business in St. Louis and join them. Two new members joined the expedition at St. Charles, although they may have been recruited earlier. One was Pierre Cruzatte; half-French and half-American Indian, he was an experienced boatman. Although blind in one eye and able to see none too well out of the other, he would usually take up the important position of bowman on the keelboat, guiding the boat through the many hidden dangers the river held. He was also valued by other expedition members for his skill in playing the fiddle. The other new recruit was François Labiche, also half-French and half-American Indian, who would serve the expedition as a translator in addition to his regular duties.

Lewis rejoined the party on May 20, and the following day, at half past three, the expedition pushed off up the Missouri. Over the next few days they passed a few small farms scattered along the riverside, including the settlement in present-day St. Charles County, Missouri, where Daniel Boone, the legendary American frontiersman, had moved to in 1799. Even these first days of travel, despite being so close to white settlements, were not without their dangers. In fact, the expedition might have come to an abrupt end on May 23, when Lewis decided to explore the edge of a rocky embankment towering some 300 feet (91 m) above the Missouri. He lost his footing at its very top and slid 20 feet (6 m) downward before catching himself by jamming his knife into a crack in the rock. A few more feet and he would have gone tumbling down to the rocks and water below.

SETTLING INTO ROUTINE

The Corps of Discovery averaged about 15 miles (24 km) a day on the Missouri that summer. Each day Clark noted in his journal the direction the river traveled through its many twists and turns, and the distance covered. Clark tended to underestimate distances traveled by river, and overestimate distances traveled by land, but on the whole the records left in the journals proved remarkably accurate when rechecked by geographers and historians in later years.

The men were usually up at first light, about 5 A.M. They would eat a hasty breakfast, strike their tents, and be on the river soon after. On most days that they were traveling, Clark would stay with the boats, while Lewis usually roamed the shore on foot. Sometimes they got lucky and their sails could propel them upstream: "The wind favourable today," Clark noted happily on May 26, "we made 18 miles [28 km]." Sometimes a back eddy in the river's current would carry them upstream, while the men rested from their efforts. But usually their progress came at the expense of hard human labor: rowing, poling, or even getting out and pulling the boats upstream with towropes, while the Missouri's fast-flowing waters tried to sweep them back down the river to St. Louis. After a day's travel, they would halt (by a convenient creek if they could find one), unload the goods they needed for the night, pitch their tents, and prepare the one hot meal they would enjoy during the day.

THE "BARKING SQUIRIL"

The strangeness of the animal population on the Great Plains added to the explorers' sense of wonder as they encountered this new landscape. On September 7, Lewis and Clark came across a burrowing animal unlike any they had ever seen before. It lived in what Clark described as a "village" containing "great numbers of holes on the top of which those little animals Set erect . . ." When Lewis and Clark approached them, they made "a Whistleing noise" before slipping into their holes. Lewis called this creature a "barking squiril," but it was Sergeant John Ordway who came up with the name for them that would catch on: *prairie dogs*. The Corps of Discovery spent the better part of the day trying to capture one by flushing out its burrow with kettles of water. They finally succeeded, and the "barking squiril" miraculously survived and was sent east to be viewed by Thomas Jefferson in the White House a year later.

According to Lewis's journal, the Great Plains were covered by herds of game in 1804. The Corps of Discovery depended on pronghorn antelope and buffalo for nourishment and hides. By 1870, overhunting by settlers, railroad workers, and game hunters had greatly diminished this source of food.

Game was abundant, and they ate heartily, consuming as much as eight or nine pounds a day per man. The deer steaks, pronghorn antelope steaks, buffalo steaks, or whatever meat the hunters happened to bring in that day would be supplemented by grapes, plums, berries, and greens picked along the way, flat bread made from cornmeal or flour, and salt pork if the hunters were not successful. On the Fourth of July in 1804, which they celebrated in present-day Atchison County, Kansas, near the mouth of the Kansas River, they marked the occasion not only with whiskey but also with cannon fire. Generally, however, the evenings were times of quiet relaxation and early bedtimes. Everyone knew that another day's hard labor awaited them when the sun rose in the morning.

The aches and pains of hard physical labor were made worse by the unending assault of stinging insects. Lewis had had the foresight to include mosquito netting in the expedition's supplies, and the men smeared grease over their exposed skin to keep off bloodsucking pests, but such preventive measures were only partially successful. "The Ticks & Musquiters are verry troublesome," Clark reported on June 17, in what became a constant refrain in his journal. Other ailments added to the misery of aches, pains, and mosquito bites, with many suffering from boils on their skin or stomach troubles. Clark in his journal attributed such ills to drinking the river water, but they were probably the product of badly preserved meat and too few fruits and vegetables in their diet. Clark had difficulty shaking a bad cold and sore throat he developed in mid-June.

The worst medical crisis the expedition would face came in late summer. Sergeant Charles Floyd had not been feeling well for several weeks. Then on August 19, Clark noted in his journal that "Serjean Floyd is taken verry bad all at once with a Biliose Chorlick [a 'bilious colic,' a term then used to describe malaria]." Clark stayed up most of that night with Floyd, ministering to him as best he could. The following day, he had sad news to record in his journal: "Sgt. Floyd died with a great deal of composure; before his death he Said to me, 'I am going away. I want you to write me a letter.'" Floyd's "bilious colic" was in all likelihood a ruptured appendix, a condition that was untreatable in the early nineteenth century, even by skilled doctors. Floyd, a native of Kentucky, was among the first to join the Corps of Discovery and was, in Clark's estimate, "[a] man of much merit." He was just 22 years old when he died. He was buried with full military honors on a hill overlooking the Missouri River in present-day Sioux City, Iowa. The men called it "Floyd's Bluff," the name by which it is still known.

The disciplinary problems that had plagued the expedition in winter camp were still evident those first months on the river. The way that Lewis and Clark dealt with such problems serves as a reminder that the Corps of Discovery was a military unit moving through hostile territory and not a group of friends out on an extended camping trip. On June 29, the captains convened a court-martial to hear the case of Privates John Collins and Hugh Hall, accused of tapping the expedition's whiskey barrel the night before, with the result that Collins was drunk while on guard. The court was made up of Sergeant Pryor and five enlisted men. Collins, who had behaved badly at St. Charles just six weeks earlier, was sentenced to 100 lashes, while Hall got 50 lashes. The entire party assembled at 3 P.M. to watch the sentence carried out. The beaten men had to go right back to work, with their bloody backs, rowing, poling, and hauling the keelboat upstream. It was a harsh punishment, but one that must have seemed right to the rest of the Corps of Discovery: A drunken guard endangered all their lives. They also knew that there was going to be no tavern along the next several thousand miles where they would be able to replenish their supply of whiskey when it ran out. Collins and Hall had enjoyed themselves at the expense of their fellow expedition members.

Private Alexander Willard faced a court-martial July 12 after Sergeant Ordway had discovered him lying asleep while on guard duty the previous night. Lewis and Clark themselves served as the court; under the military's Articles of War, Willard could have been sentenced to death by firing squad. The two captains found Willard guilty as charged and sentenced him to 100 lashes on his bare back. Private Moses Reed deserted on August 4. He was brought in alive on August 17, sentenced to run the gauntlet four times (which meant being beaten with willow switches by the entire party), and removed from the permanent party in disgrace. Finally, Private John Newman was court-martialed on October 13 for statements "of a highly criminal and mutinous nature," found guilty, and sentenced to 75 lashes and dishonorable discharge from the army and the expedition (though he, like Moses Reed, would, of necessity, accompany them to the winter encampment).

AMERICAN INDIAN DIPLOMACY

In his letter of instructions to Lewis in June 1803, Thomas Jefferson had assigned many missions to the Corps of Discovery. Beyond finding the Northwest Passage, none was as important as the assignment to establish friendly relations with the American Indian tribes living along the Missouri River and beyond. Before Lewis and Clark's journey was over, they would come in contact with nearly 50 different American Indian tribes, some of whom had never before seen a white man, let alone an American soldier.

The American West was a blank slate as far as white-American Indian relations were concerned. Although neither Western Indians nor white Americans had proven themselves especially peace-loving in the past, there had never been an armed conflict between the groups. If initial contacts were properly handled, there never need be one. On the other hand, no one could predict how the Western Indian tribes would react to the appearance of white strangers, however "friendly & conciliatory" their manner. If faced with superior force, Jefferson urged Lewis to return home rather than risk the loss of his own life and the life of his men in a losing battle: "In the loss of yourselves, we should lose also the information you will have acquired. . . . we wish you to err on the side of your safety . . ."

Lewis and Clark knew from the information they had been given before setting out that once they reached the Platte they could expect to find villages of Otoe (Oto), Missouri, and other American Indian tribes living nearby. On July 28, George Drouillard met a Missouri Indian, who told him that a mixed village of Otoe and Missouri could be found a few days travel inland. The captains dispatched the French engagé named La Liberté, the only Otoe speaker on the expedition, to establish contact with the village.

Two days later the Corps of Discovery raised an American flag on a pole and waited below a high bluff overlooking the Missouri, at a site near present-day Fort Calhoun, Nebraska. What they did not know was that La Liberté had taken advantage of his orders to abandon the expedition. Eventually, Private George Gibson was dispatched to see what had become of La Liberté and the American Indian delegation. Finally at sunset on August 2, a French trader named Mr. Fairfong arrived at the expedition's camp, accompanied by a party of Otoe and Missouri Indians. "Capt. Lewis & myself met those Indians," Clark noted, "& informed them we were glad to See them, and would Speak to them tomorrow, Sent them Som rosted meat Pork flour & meal, in return they sent us Water millions [melons]."

The next day they met the American Indian chiefs on the embankment that Lewis and Clark named Council Bluff. With Fairfong serving as translator, the captains went through a round of diplomatic gestures that would soon become routine. First they offered the American Indians presents, "in perpotion [proportion] to their Consiqunce," as Clark would write. The bigger the chief, in other words, the better the present. This could create problems if the captains misjudged just who was the biggest chief, but on this occasion they seemed to have guessed right. There was one important Otoe chief missing, named Little Thief. They

This medal is one of many distributed by the U.S. government to American Indian leaders as gestures of "peace and friendship." The side shown above is the profile portrait of Thomas Jefferson. The other side has clasped hands and a crossed tomahawk and peace pipe. The Jefferson peace medal was the first to carry the image of an American president.

sent him a bundle of clothing, an American flag, and a Jefferson peace medal (a small medallion, specially produced for the expedition, which showed Thomas Jefferson's likeness on one side, and two clasped hands superimposed on the words "Peace and Friendship" on the other). They smoked a peace pipe with the American Indian chiefs, and offered each a drink of whiskey. Lewis fired off his air gun, which much "astonished the nativs," according to Clark.

The main event, however, was Lewis's speech. Lewis spoke of Jefferson. He called Jefferson the "Great Chief of the Seventeen great nations of America." He told the American Indians that they "should obey the commands of this great chief; he has accordingly adopted them as his children." Lewis continues, saying that Jefferson "sent us out to clear the road, remove every obstruction, and to make it the road of peace between himself and his red children residing there."

Lewis promised peace, friendship, trade, and prosperity, if the Otoe and Missouri would follow the good advice of the representatives of the great chief of the seventeen American nations. What Lewis's listeners made of this speech is hard to tell. The captains perceived that they were in full agreement with its sentiments. "Those people express great Satisfa[ct]ion at the Speech Delivered," Clark wrote that evening.

On August 19, further up the Missouri, they met another party of Otoe and Missouri. This party included Little Thief and a Missouri chief named Big Horse. Once again Lewis gave his speech and showed off the gun. The present giving did not work out quite as well this time. Big Horse felt he had been honored less than had Little Thief. The Otoe and Missouri also wanted to know how much of the rich treasure trove found in the expedition's three boats would be passed on to them. Clark's description of the outcome of this council was less glowing than the one he had written two weeks before. The American Indians, obviously displeased, hung around the camp long after the captains had politely suggested they go away and "beged much for wishey [whiskey]."

On August 30, at Calumet Bluff, near the present-day site of Gavins Point Dam in Nebraska, they held their third council. This time they met with chiefs of the Yankton Nakota Sioux tribe. Jefferson had stressed the importance of making "a friendly impression" on the Sioux, "because of their immense power." The Sioux were composed of the Dakota, Lakota, and Nakota. They were further divided into numerous groups speaking separate languages. The Yankton Nakota occupied a region between the Missouri River and Minnesota. Though buffalo hunters, they also maintained some semi-permanent villages. They were used to white traders coming up the Missouri and gave Lewis and Clark a friendly reception.

Pierre Dorion, a French trader who had been traveling upriver with the expedition since June, acted as translator.

The captains explained that they came not as traders but as explorers. The chiefs were pleased about the promise of the trade that would soon come their way from St. Louis. One of their chiefs agreed to travel east to Washington, D.C., the following year to meet the Great White Father. Half Moon, a Yankton chief, passed along a friendly warning to Lewis and Clark about their cousins upstream, the Teton Lakota. "I fear those nations above will not open their ears, and you cannot, I fear[,] open them." The captains realized they might need every rifle they could muster in the weeks ahead.

The Teton Lakota lived on both sides of the Missouri and ranged far to the west across the plains in hunting and raiding parties. They played a key role in the trade system of the upper Missouri River. They acquired goods from other Dakota, Lakota, and Nakota groups who had direct contact with British traders in Canada. Then the Teton traded those goods to the tribes who lived as farmers along the upper Missouri River. The prospect of white traders coming up the Missouri seemed to the Teton as an economic threat, not a welcome source of additional goods.

The next morning, the expedition nervously awaited their guests. By late morning three Teton chiefs, Black Buffalo, the Partisan, and Buffalo Medicine, had arrived. There were also several hundred Teton who came and looked down at the white men from the riverbanks. Pierre Cruzatte acted as translator. Lewis gave his speech. Then the captains ordered their men to parade by, in their dress uniforms, with their rifles on their shoulders.

Lewis and Clark decided that Black Buffalo was the Teton's most important leader. The captains presented him with a lavish offering of gifts. The other two chiefs, especially the one known as the Partisan, felt slighted by comparison. The Partisan and Buffalo Medicine became surly. The three chiefs demanded that the expedition hand over more of its goods. The captains instead invited the chiefs and some of their men onboard the keelboat.

The Partisan became "troublesome," in what Clark later described "as a Cloak for his rascally intentions." With some difficulty, the captains managed to get the chiefs off the keelboat and onboard one of the

pirogues. Clark went along. Lewis remained in command on the keelboat. As the pirogue touched land, three Teton warriors grabbed hold
of its bow cable. The Partisan pushed up against Clark and declared
that the whites could not proceed any further up river. Clark drew his
sword. Lewis ordered all of the men to arms.

The American Indians watching from the riverbanks strung their
bows and took aim at the corps. The corps had the better weapons, but
they were badly outnumbered. At any moment, anger, pride, or an itchy
trigger finger could have unleashed a hail of gunfire and arrows that
would have left many men dead on both sides. It was Black Buffalo who
prevented this from happening. He suddenly asked Clark if the women
and children of his tribe would be able to visit the keelboat. Clark agreed.
The two sides lowered their weapons and the crisis passed.

The next day, at Black Buffalo's invitation, they visited his village.
All that day and long into the night there was feasting and speeches and
dancing. It was several days later before the expedition stopped watching the shore nervously for a Teton ambush. The Teton Lakota, Clark
declared, were "the pirates of the Missouri." He predicted nothing but
trouble with them in the future.

On October 8, the Corps of Discovery encountered a tribe more
to their liking. The Arikara were farmers growing corn and tobacco.
They lived in earthen lodges in permanent settlements. "All Tranquil-
lity," Clark recorded in his journal after three days in the company of
the Arikara. Good relations were furthered by presence of a good interpreter, Joseph Gravelines. Gravelines was a French fur trader who had
been living with the Arikara. Lewis gave his speech, gifts were distributed, and peace pipes were smoked.

THE MANDAN VILLAGES

On October 12, the Corps of Discovery set off once again up the Missouri. The weather was turning cold. Clark, suffering from rheumatism,
felt its effects cruelly. They were behind schedule. The captains decided
that they would not be able to travel farther than the known and mapped
portion of the Missouri before making their winter encampment.

On October 24, it snowed a little in the morning. Clark's rheumatism felt a bit improved. Later that day, Lewis and Clark met a Mandan
chief named Sheheke, or Big White. They met "with great Cordiallity &

Sermony [ceremony]." They smoked a peace pipe on shore. Later they invited Sheheke and his brother aboard the keelboat "for a few minits."

The next day, October 25, other Mandan rode downriver on horseback to marvel at the sight of the non-American Indian newcomers. "Indeed," Clark wrote in his journal, "they are continuelly in Sight Satisfying their Curriossities as to our apperance &c. [etc.]" The trees along the river were now bare of leaves.

On October 26, they arrived at Sheheke's village, known as Mitunka. They made their camp nearby. The Mandan were delighted at the arrival of the expedition. Never before had such a large party of non-American Indians come up the river to the Mandan villages. "Many men women Children flocked down to See us," Clark wrote in his journal. Clark's rheumatism was acting up again. He stayed at the keelboat while Lewis walked to the village with Sheheke. Other Mandan chiefs came to smoke peace pipes with Clark and marveled at the men's possessions. All in all, things were going well. The Corps of Discovery had traveled 1,600 miles (2,574 km) up the Missouri since setting off under that "jentle brease" nearly five and a half months earlier. They could go no further in 1804. The Mandan would be their neighbors until spring returned.

4

"The Most Perfect Harmoney"
Winter at Fort Mandan

SINCE THE EARLY EIGHTEENTH CENTURY, THE MANDAN VILLAGES had been one of the only native settlements along the upper Missouri River known to Europeans and white Americans. They were the most important permanent community of American Indians that the Corps of Discovery would encounter on their journey. The villages were the center of a vast trading network. It stretched across much of the northern half of the Louisiana Territory.

The Mandan lived in two villages. The southernmost of these, located on the west bank of the Missouri, was called Mitutanka. She-heke was its chief. Further up the river, on the east bank, was the second Mandan village, Nuptadi. Its chief was Black Cat. To the west, along the banks of the Knife River, lay three Hidatsa villages. The important Hidatsa chiefs included Black Moccasin and Le Borgne, also known as One Eye. In 1804, about 4,500 members of the Mandan and Hidatsa tribes lived in the five villages. In comparison, 4,000 people lived in Washington, D.C.

The villagers lived in dome-shaped earthen lodges clustered together for protection. Fields in which the people grew corn and other crops surrounded each village. The tribes spoke distinct languages, and differed in other important ways. The Mandan rarely ventured far from their home villages. Hidatsa warriors, however, ventured out on raiding parties hundreds of miles to the west. They even traveled as far as the headwaters of the Missouri, on the eastern slopes of a distant mountain range.

The Mandan lived along the banks of the Missouri River in present-day North Dakota. They lived in permanent villages of round, earthen lodges that surrounded an open plaza. When the Corps of Discovery settled in a nearby fort for the winter of 1804–1805, the Mandan supplied the men with food in exchange for trade goods.

PROMISES OF PEACE AND TRADE

As always, when they encountered new tribes, Lewis and Clark set up a formal council meeting. They hired a locally based French-Canadian trader, René Jessaume, as interpreter. Jessaume had lived among the Mandan and Arikara for many years, and he had a Mandan wife. On October 29, at a site across the Missouri from the Mandan village of Mitutanka, Mandan and Hidatsa leaders assembled to hear what the white strangers had to say. The captains made the usual speeches and presented the usual medals. Lewis fired the air gun, which drew the usual astonished response. An Arikara Indian had come up the Missouri with Lewis and Clark as a peace delegate. He pledged his tribe's peaceful intentions for the future. The Mandan generally avoided war-

THE TRADING NETWORK OF THE PLAINS INDIANS

The tribes who lived in more or less permanent agricultural villages along the Missouri River, including the Mandan, Hidatsa, Arikara, Pawnee, Wichita, and Omaha, were linked to the nomadic, buffalo-hunting groups such as the Lakota and Nakota Sioux in a vast and intricate trade network. The nomadic tribes would bring buffalo hides to annual gatherings at the agricultural villages to trade for food and tobacco, and for manufactured goods that came down from Canada and up from St. Louis. Just how far-reaching this trade extended became clear to the captains when they were returning from the Pacific in 1806 and found one of the battle axes that John Shields had manufactured at Fort Mandan in the winter of 1805 in the hands of the Nez Perce Indians, on the western side of the Rockies.

In the "Estimate of the Eastern Indians," which the captains sent back to Washington in spring 1805, they offered a detailed description of how the Mandan Indians fit in to the plains trading network. The Mandan, they wrote,

> live in fortified villages . . . and cultivate corn, beans, squashes and tobacco, which form articles of traffic with their American Indians the Assiniboin [a Canadian tribe]: they also barter horses with the Assiniboins for arms, ammunition, axes, kettles, and other articles of European manufacture, which these last obtain from the British establishments on the Assiniboin river.

The Mandan then bartered the European goods for horses and "leather tents" (by which they probably meant buffalo skins), from Western Indian tribes, including the Crow and Cheyenne "who visit them occasionally for the purpose of traffic."

European (and, increasingly, American) goods such as muskets, iron pots, metal fishhooks, and woven cloth made life easier for the American Indians in this trade network. But they also encouraged a new and more wasteful attitude toward natural resources as American Indians began to overhunt their territories for the animal hides and furs valued by the Europeans.

fare. They would have liked to believe their southern flank was now secure from attack. However they remained skeptical about the value of promises offered by "liars and bad men" like the Arikara.

Lewis and Clark's promises of trade goods coming up the Missouri from St. Louis sparked genuine enthusiasm, particularly among the Mandan. More traders bringing more goods would work to the economic advantage of the Mandan. Black Cat and Big White, the principal Mandan chiefs, invited Lewis and Clark to spend the winter. To improve their own position with the Americans, the Mandan spread rumors among the Hidatsa that the whites were up to no good. The Americans, they claimed, were even planning an attack on their villages in alliance with the Sioux. While Black Cat and Big White frequently visited the captains that winter, the Hidatsa chiefs stayed away.

WINTER QUARTERS

By November 3, the men of the corps began constructing a fort. It would be their winter home. Sergeant Patrick Gass, the expedition's master carpenter, left a detailed description of its design and construction in his journal.

> *The following is the manner in which our fort and huts were built; the huts were in two rows, containing four rooms each, and joined at one end forming an angle. When rasied [raised] about 7 feet high a floor of [split planks] were laid, and covered with grass and clay; which made a warm loft. The upper part [of the huts] projected a foot over and the roofs were made shed-fashion, rising from the inner side, and making the outer wall about 18 feet high . . . In the angle formed by the two rows of huts we built two rooms, for holding our provisions and stores.*

The fort was home that winter to 35 soldiers. The next spring, Lewis and Clark and 26 enlisted men would go west. Corporal Warfington and six soldiers would take the keelboat back to St. Louis. A number of civilians would also live in the fort, including York, Drouillard, and Jessaume and his Mandan wife. One of the fort's inhabitants was a French trapper they met at the Mandan villages, Jean-Baptiste Lepage. He had traveled a few dozen miles farther up the Missouri. The captains persuaded him to become part of the permanent party that would set out westward the following spring.

By the last week of November, the men were sleeping under the roofs of their newly completed huts. Snow was beginning to fall regularly. Clark recorded 13 inches on the ground November 29. By the first week of December the Missouri River was covered with ice. The keelboat and pirogues were frozen at the water's edge. No matter what happened, there was no retreat now until spring came.

The days were short. The winter sun provided little warmth. On December 7, Clark recorded in his journal that the temperature was 44 degrees "below Breizing [freezing]" in the morning (or 12 degrees below zero). Before the winter was over it would get a lot colder, down to -42° F (-41° C). With few trees to block the wind blowing down from the Canadian prairies, the wind chill effect could have deadly consequences. "Our rooms are verry close and warm," Sergeant Ordway wrote of the huts in the fort, "So we can keep ourselves warm and comfortable, but the Sentinel who stood out in the open weather had to be relieved every hour. . . ." Any trip outside could have painful consequences. Toes, fingers, and ears froze. The captains soon became expert at treating frostbite.

When the men were not on duty, they played backgammon or socialized with the American Indians. The American Indian visitors came to witness the curious novelty of a large number of white men living together in their midst. When darkness fell, Cruzatte brought out his fiddle to entertain the expedition members and their guests. As Clark noted in his journal toward the end of the winter, "fiew nights pass without a Dance." The heavens also provided some entertainment; the men were treated to a display of the northern lights in November. A total eclipse of the moon occurred in January.

Discipline was not a problem at Fort Mandan. The captains had established their authority over the men and won their loyalty. There was only one court-martial, of a man who climbed over the wall of the fort rather than ask to be admitted at the gate. Though he was sentenced to 50 lashes, the sentence was never carried out. That would prove the last court-martial Lewis and Clark convened. At winter's end, Lewis would be able to write proudly to Jefferson:

every individual of the party are in good health, and excellent sperits; zealously attatched to the enterprise, and anxious to proceed; not a whisper of discontent or murmur is to be heard among them; but all in unison, act with the most perfect harmoney. With such men I have every thing to hope, and but little to fear.

While the enlisted men carried out the routine tasks of garrison duty, the captains had their own business to attend to. Lewis and Clark realized that the Hidatsa had felt slighted by them since their arrival. They worried that the Hidatsa would favor the British traders over potential U.S. rivals. In late November, Lewis went up to the Hidatsa villages to win them over. He handed out gifts and assured the Hidatsa chiefs that the expedition's intentions were strictly peaceful. Trade with the Americans, he assured the Hidatsa, would work to the benefit of both the Mandan and their tribe.

Lewis and Clark also needed to build a relationship with the British traders who came down from Canada to do business with the Mandan and Hidatsa. Lewis had not forgiven the British for his father's death in the Revolution. But, along with Clark, he assured the traders that they were still welcome to do business with the tribes along the Missouri River. However, they did insist that the British should no longer hand out medals or the British flag as gifts to the American Indians. Lewis and Clark believed doing so would only confuse the tribes as to which Great White Father ruled their land. Lewis and Clark wanted no more American Indian chiefs in the Louisiana Territory wearing medals bearing the likeness of King George.

The British traders did not challenge U.S. authority. They actually provided the captains with some valuable services. Clark noted in his journal in mid-December that a trader named Hugh Heney had given them "Some Scetches of the Countery between the Mississippi & Missouri." Even more importantly, Heney gave them sketches "which he had obtained from the Indins, to the *West* of this place."

TAKING STOCK

In spring Corporal Warfington and his men would take the keelboat back to St. Louis. This was the last chance Lewis and Clark would have to communicate with President Jefferson until their own return from the Pacific. They began to set down a detailed account of all that they had learned on their journey thus far up the Missouri River.

Clark reviewed his journal entries. He drew up the most accurate map yet available of the wandering trail of the Missouri River between St. Louis and the Mandan villages. Lewis wrote out a "summary view of the rivers and creeks which discharge themselves into the Missouri . . ."

Lewis and Clark prepared to send back samples of 108 types of plants and seeds. They packed up samples of 68 types of minerals they had dug out along the shoreline of the Missouri. They also prepared samples of the animals they had encountered. These included bones, horns, animal hides, and a few live specimens of smaller and more transportable creatures, including a prairie dog, which must have spent a boring winter in its little cage. They boxed up Clark's journal. It, too, would go back as a record of their own efforts since first proceeding on up the Missouri.

Lewis and Clark prepared vocabulary lists of several American Indian languages. They assembled for shipment samples of American Indian material culture. These included weapons, pottery, and buffalo fur robes. They wrote a report entitled "Estimate of Eastern Indians." Here they summarized all that they had learned of dozens of American Indian tribes and bands living along the Missouri. They reported on the location of the various tribes, their economies, their customs, their attitudes toward whites, and their relations with other American Indians. Jefferson thought so highly of the "estimate" when he received it late in 1805 that he had it reprinted as an official report to Congress the following year.

RAIDS AND CELEBRATIONS

The winter routine at Fort Mandan was interrupted on several occasions by dramatic events. The first occurred at the end of November. A Mandan man brought news that Lakota Sioux and Arikara warriors had attacked a Mandan hunting party. They left one hunter dead, two wounded, and stole nine horses. Lewis and Clark decided that a show of military strength was called for. With 21 armed men, Clark set off across the frozen Missouri to offer his services to the Mandan. He planned to hunt down the Lakota Sioux and Arikara war party.

The Mandan would have none of it. They knew what it meant to go chasing out over the plains through deep snow in the dead of winter. Vengeance could wait until the spring. Clark and his men, probably a little embarrassed by the whole episode, returned to the fort. On February 14 a group of men from the fort, led by George Drouillard, headed south to bring in some meat killed by an earlier hunting party. A much larger band of Lakota Sioux stole two of their three horses as well as a couple of knives. It seems that the Lakota Sioux wanted to send a message about who really was in charge along the Missouri. Lewis set out with a party of American soldiers and some Mandan warriors to attack the raiders. After chasing them over 30 miles of frozen landscape, they gave up. The Americans had no more encounters with Teton Lakota Sioux that winter. When spring came the expedition would leave its territory far behind.

Christmas and the New Year brought happier diversions. On Christmas Eve, Lewis and Clark distributed flour, dried apples, and pepper. These were rare treats. New Year's Day brought another round of celebrations. The captains ordered the cannon fired at the fort to mark the occasion. Then, at the invitation of the Mandan in Mituntaka, Clark and 16 of the expedition members visited the village. They brought a fiddle, a tambourine, and a horn. Moving from one earthen lodge to the next, they danced with the Mandan for much of the day.

GETTING READY FOR SPRING

In February, Lewis and Clark prepared for their spring departure. The men chopped the boats free of the river ice. They hauled them ashore and began to make repairs. In early March they cut down and began hollowing out cottonwood trees to make six dugout canoes. These would replace the large keelboat that Corporal Warfington would return to St. Louis. Soon the river ice began to break up. Clark was impressed by the "extraordinary dexterity" of the American Indians, as they jumped from one ice floe to another. Lewis and Clark resolved to be on their way westward the first week in April. The American Indians had sketched maps of the western Missouri for them. The contributions of the Hidatsa were particularly helpful. They had traveled as far west as the Rocky Mountains.

Lewis and Clark understood for the first time that the Missouri did not simply travel in a straight line west after leaving the Mandan villages. They would have more miles to travel along the winding course of the river than they had originally thought. Thanks to the Hidatsa, they now knew the approximate distance to the various large rivers emptying into the Missouri.

The Hidatsa gave them valuable directions too. They learned about an unmistakable landmark, the Great Falls of the Missouri. The Corps would have to portage their canoes and supplies around the falls. This detour, they were assured, was no more than a half mile. As they neared the Rocky Mountains they would come to three forks in the river. They were to take the westernmost fork, which would lead them up and over the mountains. Here they would pass the headwaters of the Missouri and cross over the Continental Divide. On the other side, after another short portage, they would come to the headwaters of what was described to them as the south fork of the Columbia River. It was this river that would lead them to the Pacific.

Clark calculated that from the Continental Divide to the Pacific would be a water journey of no more than 300 miles (482 km). He thought they could make it to the Pacific and back to the Mandan village before the next winter set in.

One of the problems with this route was getting the team's supplies across the Rockies. It was impossible for the men to carry everything on their backs. They decided to purchase horses from the Shoshone Indians. This tribe lived near the end of the Missouri. However, the Shoshone had never seen white men before. They spoke neither English nor French. Lewis and Clark, of course, spoke no Shoshone. Establishing contact with the Shoshone, explaining their mission to them, and bartering for horses might prove difficult.

SACAGAWEA JOINS THE EXPEDITION

The solution to Lewis and Clark's problem was waiting for them in one of the Hidatsa villages. A trader named Toussaint Charbonneau lived there. The captains hired him at a salary of $25 a month. Charbonneau did little to earn his pay. Lewis would later describe him as "a man of no particular merit." Charbonneau's one valuable service was bringing his teenage wife, Sacagawea, along on the expedition.

Sacagawea, pictured with Lewis and Clark, joined the expedition with her husband, Toussaint Charbonneau, as a translator among the Shoshone. The corps' journals make it clear throughout that she was a valuable part of the team. Not only did she help negotiate a trade for horses that made the passage across the Rockies possible, she saved the expedition journals from a capsized boat.

Sacagawea, whose name meant "Bird Woman" in Hidatsa, was about 15 years old in 1804. She was a Lemhi Shoshone. She was born into a band that roamed a territory around the Continental Divide in present-day southeastern Idaho and southwestern Montana. Five years earlier she had been kidnapped by Hidatsa raiders near the three forks of the Missouri River.

The captains may not have appreciated just how useful Sacagawea was going to be when they hired Charbonneau. They learned her value during the course of the winter. Sacagawea could translate from Shoshone to Hidatsa. Charbonneau could translate Hidatsa into French. One of the French speakers on the expedition could translate into English for the captains. Then the chain of translation could be reversed. When they found the Shoshone, they would have a chance of obtaining those horses.

On February 11, 1805, Sacagawea delivered a baby. Her son was named Jean-Baptiste Charbonneau, but he became better known by his nickname, Pomp. Sacagawea had seven weeks to regain her strength and nurse her new baby before it was time to go. At the start of April 1805, the Corps of Discovery had taken final form. Thirty-one men, one woman, and an infant, along with Lewis's big black Newfoundland, Seaman, were about to sail up the unknown Missouri.

5

Into the Unknown

AT 4 P.M. ON APRIL 7, 1805, THE CORPS OF DISCOVERY BEGAN THEIR journey again. This time they entered territory that no white men had ever seen. To mark the occasion, Meriwether Lewis started making regular daily entries in his journal. This was the first time he wrote in his journal regularly since September 1804. Over the next few months, he wrote some of the most famous lines in exploration literature. One famous passage was penned on April 7. "This little fleet," he wrote, meaning the expedition's white and red pirogues, plus the six new dugout canoes:

> *altho' not quite so rispectable as those of Columbus or Capt. Cook, were still viewed by us with as much pleasure as those deservedly famed adventurers ever beheld theirs. . . . We were now about to penetrate a country at least two thousand miles in width, on which the foot of civilized man had never trodden; the good or evil it had in store for us was for experiment yet to determine, and these little vessels contained every article by which we were to expect to subsist or defend ourselves.*

There was great uncertainty about what would happen once they headed into the unknown. Yet Meriwether Lewis was sure of one thing: "I could but esteem this moment of my departure as among the most happy of my life."

THE JOURNEY RESUMES

Lewis set out briskly on foot along the shore that afternoon while the rest of the corps rowed the clumsy new dugouts against the Missouri's current. Lewis walked the six miles from the fort to the second Mandan village, Nuptadi. There he hoped to say good-bye to Chief Black Cat. The chief was not there, so Lewis walked back down the river to the expedition's camp. They had traveled only three miles from their starting point. Next day's progress was little better although they were slowed by the swamping of one of the canoes and the need to stop and dry a barrel of gunpowder that had gotten soaked.

By the third day, the expedition hit its stride. The canoes journeyed nearly 24 miles (38 km) upstream. On April 10, they made nearly 19 miles (30 km). By April 12, they had reached the first major landmark Lewis and Clark had been told to watch for by the Hidatsa, the mouth of the Little Missouri River. During their last months on the river in 1804, they had traveled northward on the Missouri. Now they were at last heading more or less due west.

Lewis seemed pleased with everything he saw. He described the country as "one continuous level fertile plain as far as the eye can reach." He wrote of "extensive and extreemly fertile high plains and meadows." Little grew upon that "fertile plain," however, except short grass and sagebrush. Hardly a tree was to be seen past the river's edge. The farther west they traveled into the High Plains region, the drier the climate grew. Clark seemed less enchanted with the western countryside. Adjectives like *fertile* rarely appeared in Clark's journal descriptions of the landscape.

Game was scarce at first because hunting parties from the Mandan and Hidatsa villages had hunted most of the animals during the long winter. The expedition traveled for four days before Drouillard and Clark finally killed a deer. Sacagawea helped provide food by gathering wild Jerusalem artichokes. The river was home to a large population of bird life, including brant, geese, swans, gulls, ducks, and whooping cranes. When Clark killed a goose on April 13, Lewis climbed to the top of "a lofty cottonwood tree" to collect an egg from its nest, but whether out of scientific curiosity or hunger for fried egg he did not say.

The Corps of Discovery enjoyed returning to the routine of river travel. Each morning, one of the captains would take up position as

Throughout the expedition, Lewis and Clark wrote in their journals about the people and unfamiliar plants and animals they encountered. They recorded nearly 300 kinds of plants and animals that had been unknown to science. This illustration is one that Clark made of the sage grouse, a bird Lewis dubbed "mountain cock," "heath cock," and "cock of the plains."

commander of the little fleet. He rode in the white pirogue. The other captain—more often than not, Lewis—would walk along the shore. After their nightly meal, Cruzatte would break out his fiddle.

Each night, Lewis and Clark would sit by the campfire and write in their journals. The captains, Charbonneau, Sacagawea, and Drouillard slept in a tipi (or teepee) of "dressed Buffaloe skins." This was one of the few instances on the expedition in which rank obviously had its privileges. The enlisted men slept in the open. Their old enemies, the mosquitoes, were in evidence early on. "I saw a Musquetor today," Clark wrote on April 9.

By the second week out, they no longer had to worry about food. "I saw Several Small parties of antelope," Clark recorded in his journal of April 17, "large herds of Elk. . . . also a Beaver house." Clark killed a buffalo and four deer while walking alone along the shore on April 21. That same day, Lewis and a group of men killed three deer, two beavers, and four buffalo calves. The young buffalo, Lewis noted, were "very delicious . . . equal to any veal I ever tasted." He also wrote approvingly of the taste of beaver tail and beaver liver. The men killed for food, not for sport, and little went to waste. To feed the 33 members of the expedition, the hunters needed to bring in four deer or antelope or one buffalo every day. If they had too much fresh meat for immediate consumption, they cut the surplus into small strips and dried it. They kept this jerky for days when the hunters were less successful.

Through April and into May, the expedition had to fight against high winds blowing eastward. Their progress was slow. The wind severely tested the boat-handling skills of the Corps of Discovery. Some men were found wanting. On April 13, Touissant Charbonneau steered the white pirogue. This was the expedition's most important boat now. It carried medicine, trade goods, and the captains' journals. It also carried Sacagawea, Pomp, and several nonswimmers among the soldiers. Disaster loomed when the wind's direction shifted suddenly, and Charbonneau made a mistake at the rudder. The white pirogue nearly tipped over. With Lewis shouting orders, Drouillard seized the rudder from the hapless Charbonneau. Other men took down the sails. The boat and its precious cargo were saved.

The wind made everyone miserable. Windblown sand inflamed eyes and gummed up the works of Lewis's pocket watch. "We are compelled to eat, drink, and breathe it . . ." he complained on April 24.

WHERE NO WHITE MAN
HAD BEEN BEFORE

Despite the hardships of the journey, the travelers were sustained by pride in their accomplishments. Every mile they sailed westward, they knew they were making history. On April 14, a week out from the Mandan villages, they reached a small creek running into the Missouri. They named it after Charbonneau. Given that this was the same man who had nearly sunk the white pirogue the day before, it may seem strange that the captains bestowed this honor upon him. Lewis explained the decision in his journal. "[W]e called [it] Sharbono's Creek, after our interpreter who encamped several weeks on it with a hunting party of Indians. This was the highest point to which any whiteman had ascended; except two Frenchmen who having lost their way had straggled a few miles further, tho' to what place precisely I could not learn." As far as Lewis knew, once the expedition had gone a few miles past Charbonneau's creek—present-day Bear Den Creek, near the McLean-Dunn county line, North Dakota—the Corps of Discovery had entered a region that no white person had ever seen before.

On April 22, they reached the White Earth River in North Dakota. This was the first of two rivers entering the Missouri from the north that the Hidatsa had told them to expect. On April 25, two and a half weeks after their departure, they came the mouth of the Yellowstone River. Eager to get to the river, Lewis had left the little fleet behind on the Missouri that morning. He hiked overland with four men and his dog, Seaman. Lewis got his first glimpse of the Yellowstone from a hilltop. He described "a most pleasing view of the country, particularly of the wide and fertile vallies formed by the missouri and the yellowstone rivers, which occasionally unmasked by the wood on their borders disclose their meanderings for many miles through these delightfull tracts of country."

The Hidatsa had praised the lush Yellowstone country. They described an abundance of furs waiting to be taken by trappers and the river's year-round navigability all the way to the foot of the Rocky Mountains. Following Jefferson's instructions, the expedition would have to stick to the Missouri River on their westward trek. However, the captains decided to include a side trip down the Yellowstone on their return.

At noon on the next day, Clark and the rest of the expedition reached the mouth of the Yellowstone. That night there was fiddle music and dancing around the campfire. The Corps celebrated reaching "this long wished for spot," as Lewis described it.

CROSSING MONTANA

On April 27, the expedition crossed the invisible line that would be the future state border between North Dakota and Montana. Those early days in the Montana wilderness were among the most blessed in the memory of the explorers. For one thing, they were feeling very well fed. Game proved so plentiful that hunting came to resemble a shopping trip. "We can send out at any time and obtain whatever species of meat the country affords in as large quantity as we wish," Lewis wrote on May 8. Sacagawea continued to prove her value to the expedition. She identified and gathered wild edible plants along the way.

Even in early May there were some snowy days. Clark described "a verry extraodernarey climate, to behold the trees Green & flowers spred on the plain, & snow an inch deep." The expedition journals also were filled with entries recording "a fine day" or "a fine morning." The scenery was a constant delight. Lewis noted on May 4 that the "country on both sides of the Missouri continues to be open level fertile and beautifull as far as the eye can reach . . ." Clark, as usual, dropped the "fertile." Even he agreed that day that the countryside was "rich high and butifull . . ."

The expedition continued to make good progress up the Missouri. The Hidatsa had told them they would encounter a major river entering the Missouri from the north. The River Which Scolds at All Others lay about 500 miles (804 km) to the west of the Mandan villages. Sure enough, on May 8, they came across its mouth. Finding the native name too much of a mouthful, they renamed it the Milk River.

The Missouri began to cut a deeper channel through the surrounding countryside. Its high, crumbling riverbanks posed a new threat to the expedition. "I sometimes wonder," Lewis wrote on May 11, "that some of our canoes or perogues are not swallowed up by means of the immence mass of earth which are eternally precipitating themselves into the river."

Human error proved more dangerous than nature. Once again Charbonneau steered the rudder of the white pirogue, and once again he proved unfit. On May 14, a sudden squall surprised the little fleet. Lewis and Clark were both on shore. This violated their usual rule that one of them should remain aboard the white pirogue. They watched as the pirogue turned broadside to the wind and began to take on water. All they could do was yell for Charbonneau to come about, or turn the boat. Lewis wrote disgustedly in his journal that night. "Charbono, still crying to his god for mercy, had not yet recollected the rudder, nor could the repeated orders of the bowsman, Cruzat, bring him to his recollection untill he threatened to shoot him instantly if he did not take hold of the rudder and do his duty . . ." Cruzatte's threat worked. Charbonneau finally grabbed the rudder and turned the boat into the wind. The men bailed the water with cooking pots, and the pirogue was saved.

Charbonneau was a disgrace. His wife, however, impressed the men with her coolheaded competence. Even Lewis, who did not yet seem to hold Sacagawea in high regard, wrote warmly of her performance that day. "The Indian woman, to whom I ascribe equal fortitude and resolution with any person on board at the time of the accident, caught and preserved most of the light articles, which were washed overboard." Her actions were all the more remarkable, considering she had to keep her infant son, Pomp, safe.

The men often had to jump into the river or scramble along the sharp stones and slippery mud of the riverbank in order to pull the boats through shallow or rapid stretches with towropes. Despite this, they made continued progress. On May 20, they reached the Musselshell River (in central Montana), another landmark they had been told to look for. On May 29, they came to another river that had gone unmentioned by the Hidatsa. Clark named it Judith's River, after Julia (Judith) Hancock, a young girl he knew back home. After his return from the expedition, Julia, by then aged 16, became his wife. Her river would in time become known as the Judith River.

SPECTACULAR LANDSCAPE

In the third week of May, snow-capped mountains appeared on the horizon. On May 17, Clark spotted some high peaks in the northwest. They were part of the Little Rocky Mountains. This range is located in north-central Montana, detached from and well east of the Rockies. On May 25 Clark noted more mountains to both the north and south of the Missouri. These were the Little Rocky and Bears Paw ranges to the north and the Judith range to the south. Clark understood that these mountains were not the long-sought Rockies described to them by the Hidatsa. In the distance, farther to the southwest, he saw another "range of high mounts." Lewis saw them the next day and instantly decided

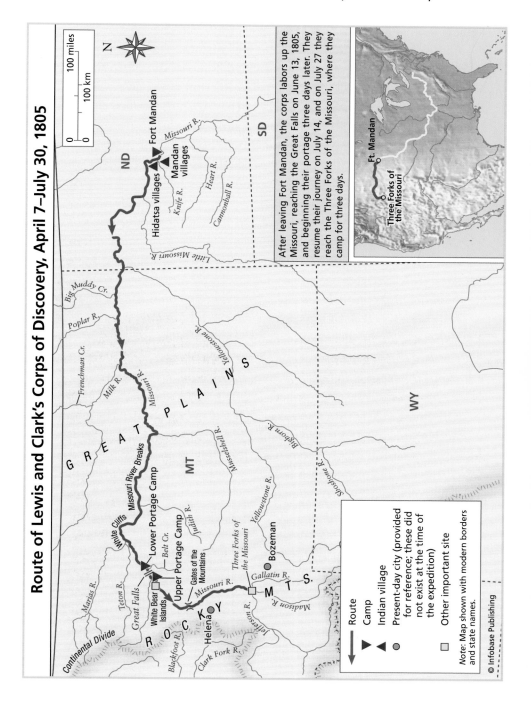

Route of Lewis and Clark's Corps of Discovery, April 7–July 30, 1805

After leaving Fort Mandan, the corps labors up the Missouri, reaching the Great Falls on June 13, 1805, and beginning their portage three days later. They resume their journey on July 14, and on July 27 they reach the Three Forks of the Missouri, where they camp for three days.

Route

Camp

Indian village

Present-day city (provided for reference; these did not exist at the time of the expedition)

Other important site

Note: Map shown with modern borders and state names.

© Infobase Publishing

they must be the Rockies. He confessed to his journal his "secret plea-sure" in arriving "so near the head of heretofore conceived boundless Missouri . . ." (In reality, the peaks hovering tantalizingly on the south-west horizon were probably the Highwood Mountains, still another detached range, and not part of the Rockies.)

The mountains were spectacular but distant. The river was now lined with hills and bluffs. They provided some of the most amazing scenery the expedition had yet seen. This section of the river was later called the Missouri Breaks. In parts of the Missouri Breaks, the river cuts deeply through layers of shale and sandstone. The towering cliffs on either side of the river had eroded over hundreds of thousands of years into fantastic shapes. Lewis described it as a kind of dream land-scape. In another of the famous journal entries he made that spring, Lewis wrote of the White Cliffs:

> *The water in the course of time in decending from those hills and plains on either side of the river has trickled down the soft sand cliffs and woarn it into a thousand grotesque figures, which with the help of a little immagination and an oblique view, at a distance are made to represent eligant ranges of lofty freestone buildings, having their parapets well stocked with statuary; coll-umns of various sculptures both grooved and plain, are also seen supporting long galleries in front of those buildings. . .*

On June 2, still within the Missouri Breaks, they came to the mouth of another, unexpected river. This one posed a problem. It entered the Missouri from the north. From what the Hidatsa had told Lewis and Clark, the last major northern tributary of the Missouri was the River Which Scolds at All Others. Lewis and Clark thought they had already passed this river. Was this then the real Scolding River? Was it another river? Or was it a fork in the Missouri that the Hidatsa had not men-tioned? If it was a fork, which river would lead them to the Rockies?

In reality they had stumbled across an entirely separate river. Had spring rains upstream not swelled it, they never would have mistaken it for a fork of the mighty Missouri. The captains needed to make sure. From June 3 through June 12, the expedition camped at the junction of the two rivers. This place was later known as Decision Point.

By the next day, Lewis and Clark had a strong hunch that the southern "fork" was the real Missouri. The northern river was muddier than the southern. The captains believed this meant it flowed through open plains. The clearer southern river probably flowed out of the mountains. Most of the enlisted men, however, were not persuaded by the captains' argument.

Taking the wrong fork now would mean delay or even worse. To "mistake the stream at this period of the season . . ." Lewis wrote in his journal on June 3, "and to ascend such stream to the rocky Mountain or perhaps much further before we could inform ourselves whether it did approach the Columbia or not, and then be obliged to return and take the other stream would not only loose us the whole of the season but would probably so dishearten the party that it might defeat the expedition altogether." The fate of the Corps of Discovery rested on the decision Lewis and Clark would now make.

Clark led a party up the southern river far enough to spot more snow-capped mountains in the distance, known as the Little Belt and Big Belt ranges (a segment of the northern Rocky Mountains in central Montana). The party determined that the river headed in the southwesterly direction described by the Hidatsa. Lewis, meanwhile, led a party 40 miles up the northern river. Although it headed west from its juncture with the Missouri, it soon bent northward. Lewis was now certain that he and Clark had been right in their earlier hunch. This northern river was not the Missouri. Lewis named the northern river Maria's River after his cousin Maria Wood.

Lewis and Clark were now certain in their own minds as to how to proceed. Their men remained unconvinced. Lewis could have ordered them back into the boats to follow his and Clark's lead. This was his right as commander. He decided that it was more important for everyone to be in agreement on their course, even at the cost of a few more days' delay. If he could find the Great Falls of the Missouri along the southern river, there could no longer be any question as to the direction they should follow.

THE GREAT FALLS OF THE MISSOURI

On June 11, Lewis, Drouillard, and three others set out up the southern river. Lewis had been suffering from violent stomach cramps and a fever for several days. His progress was slow. That night, he had his men brew up a medicinal concoction of boiled chokecherry twigs. He swallowed the brew, and it seemed to work. He felt better the next day.

On the morning of June 13, Lewis walked along the prairie, high above the river. He spotted what looked like smoke in the distance. He heard a deep roaring noise. Lewis was seeing the spray and hearing the sound of falling waters. Seven miles farther on, a "sublimely grand specticle" awaited the explorers. They peered down at the magnificent Great Falls. Lewis climbed down from the prairie's edge to the foot of the falls. For the next four hours he sat transfixed by the scene, "the grandest sight I ever beheld."

The next day Joseph Field set off, carrying a letter from Lewis to Clark reporting on the discovery. Lewis began to scout out the portage that lay ahead. He soon discovered that the Great Falls was actually five sets of falls, stretching over 10 miles (16 km) of river. The trip around the falls would require an extremely long portage. The water route to the Pacific was taking on unexpected complications.

Lewis's adventures were not over for the day. He shot a buffalo for his supper. As he approached his fallen prey with a now empty gun, he spotted a grizzly. Lewis started to retreat. The grizzly headed straight toward him. In desperation, Lewis waded waist-deep into the Missouri. He turned to face the bear. This time it was the bear that flinched. It turned and fled. Reloading his rifle (and vowing never to neglect that precaution again), Lewis went back to reclaim the dead buffalo. Then he saw another fearsome-looking creature of the "tiger kind" (possibly a wolverine). Lewis decided "all the beasts of the neighborhood had made a league to distroy me." He gave up his plan to spend the night alone on the prairie.

As he walked back to meet the rest of his party, three buffalo bulls charged him. These "curious adventures" seemed to Lewis like something out of a tale of "inchantment." He thought it all "might be a dream," but he was reminded that he was awake and had a long way still to walk by the prickly pear spines "which pierced my feet very severely . . . ." He finally arrived back at camp long after dark. His encounters with the animal kingdom were not quite over. When he woke the next morning, he found a large rattlesnake curled up 10 feet (3 m) from where he was sleeping.

ENCOUNTERS WITH THE GRIZZLY

Montana's abundant wildlife included one new creature whose acquaintance the Corps of Discovery would have preferred not to have made: the grizzly bear. The Mandan had warned the men of the grizzly's fierceness. Lewis and Clark, however, believed that the grizzly was no match for his men and their guns.

On May 5, Clark and Drouillard encountered a grizzly. Clark described it as "a very large and turrible looking animal, which we found verry hard to kill." It took 10 musket balls, five of them shot into the bear's lungs, to bring the beast down. The bear stood well over eight feet tall and had nearly five-inch-long talons. They estimated that it weighed more than 500 pounds. Lewis adopted a more respectful tone in his journal: "I find that the curiousity of our party is pretty well satisfyed with rispect to this anamal." They may have been done with grizzlies. The grizzlies, however, were not done with them. On May 11, Private Bratton shot a grizzly through the lungs. The wounded bear chased Bratton for half a mile before giving up. Lewis sent a party out to finish off the wounded grizzly. He later confessed that he would "reather fight two Indians than one bear."

When Lewis and Clark made their journey, there may have been more than 100,000 grizzly bears roaming the area that was destined to become the lower 48 states of the United States. Today there are perhaps 1,100 left. Most live on national parkland in Montana and Wyoming.

Meanwhile, on June 12, Clark and the rest of the men had set out up the Missouri. Before leaving, they stored some supplies to recover on their return trip. In two pits, they left a half-ton of food, gunpowder, tools, and weapons. They also left behind the red pirogue, hidden beneath a pile of brush. Clark fretted about Sacagawea's health. She had been feverish and suffering stomach pain for several days. "The Interpreters woman verry Sick worse than she has been," Clark noted in his journal on the evening of June 12.

On June 14, Joseph Field met up with Clark. Field delivered the note from Lewis announcing the discovery of Great Falls. He also warned Clark that near the falls the river ran too rapidly to allow for safe passage of the boats. On June 15, the main party with Clark stopped about a mile below the falls. Lewis and his party joined them the next day. They camped near a side stream that Field had said might be used as a starting point for their portage. This camp was known as the Lower Portage camp.

THE GREAT FALLS PORTAGE

Lewis told Clark what he had seen upriver. He recommended that they follow a portage route along the river's south side. Clark agreed. He then left camp to plan the portage route.

They hid the white pirogue near the Lower Portage camp for their return trip, along with another store of supplies. The men built wooden carts. They would use these carts to drag the expedition's remaining supplies and canoes across the prairie portage. Clark returned on June 20. He suggested they make their upper camp past the mouth of the Medicine River, near what he called White Bears Island. He estimated the distance between the two camps at seventeen and three-quarter miles.

Meanwhile, Lewis took over the task of treating Sacagawea's illness. It would be a disaster if she died, he wrote. She was "our only dependence for a friendly negociation with the Snake [Shoshone] Indians on whom we depend for horses to assist us in our portage from the Missouri to the columbia river." He gave her a dose of powdered bark and opium. He also had her drink mineral water from a local spring. Within a few days she showed signs of recovery.

The corps began the portage on June 22. Lewis directed that the iron frame of his experimental boat, which they had hauled all the way from Harpers Ferry in Virginia, be included in the first load. Most of the party under Clark would cross and recross the route between Lower Portage camp and White Bears Island camp. Lewis and a smaller group would remain at the upper camp to assemble the iron boat. When completed, it would take the place of the white pirogue they had left below.

The portage route was one of the most difficult parts of the journey so far. Deep ravines frequently cut the ground. The little handmade carts were hard to push or control. They often broke down and had to be repaired. Prickly pear cactus spines cut through moccasins and punctured feet. Storms dropped hailstones the size of apples. The Corps of Discovery stumbled on, injured and exhausted. "[A]t every halt," Lewis wrote, "these poor fellows tumble down and are so much fortiegued that many of them are asleep in an instant."

Meanwhile, work went on at the upper camp assembling Lewis's experimental boat. Wood had to be cut and shaped to fill out the frame. Animal skins had to be prepared and sewn together to serve as the boat's hull. Lewis became camp cook. He prepared buffalo dumplings as a special treat for his hard-working men.

On July 2, Clark and his weary men delivered the last load of supplies. The boat was still unfinished. The men who were not working on it got a few days' rest. On July 4, they celebrated Independence Day. Lewis and Clark made a decision. They would not, as originally intended, send anyone back from the Great Falls to report to Jefferson. They were going to need every man they had for the challenges to come. They also now realized it would be impossible for the corps to reach the Pacific and return to Fort Mandan that year as previously planned. They now hoped to just make it to the Pacific in 1805.

The iron boat was ready for a trial sailing on July 9. It leaked. Lewis had counted on sealing the seams of the sewn animal skins with a tar made from pine pitch. However, no pines grew at the Great Falls. The mixture of charcoal and tallow that Lewis devised as a substitute did not work. They had lugged the iron frame across two-thirds of the North American continent for nothing. "I need not add that this circumstance mortifyed me not a little," Lewis wrote in his journal. "I bid a dieu to my boat. . . ." The failure of Lewis's cherished experiment meant another delay in setting off. To take the place of the iron boat, they had to build two more dugout canoes. This cost them five more summer travel days.

CLOSING IN ON THE ROCKIES

On July 15, the expedition once again proceeded up the Missouri. They could see the Rockies—the real Rockies this time—in the distance. The men traveled in eight dugout canoes. The river changed direction again. West of Great Falls the Missouri bent south, just as the Hidatsa had told them it would.

On July 16, they found hoofprints and willow shelters along the riverside. An American Indian party had camped there. The camp was at least a week and a half old. It was the closest they had come to encountering other human beings since shortly after their departure from the Mandan villages. Sacagawea thought the camp's inhabitants must have been from her own tribe, the Shoshone.

Lewis and Clark were eager to meet with the Shoshone people. However, they knew they would not catch up with a party of mounted Shoshone while traveling up the river in the canoes. They also feared that the sound of gunfire from their hunters' rifles would spook the Shoshone. The Shoshone might fear the shots came from a Hidatsa raiding party. On July 18, Clark, accompanied by Joseph Field, John Potts, and York, headed out overland searching for the Shoshone. Lewis remained behind in command of the expedition fleet.

On July 19, Lewis's little fleet reached a narrow, rocky gorge cut by the Missouri through the Big Belt Mountains. He named the entrance to the gorge "the Gates of the Rocky Mountains." The river twisted and turned through nearly six miles of high cliffs on either side. Clark's party rejoined the expedition on the Missouri on July 21. Clark's report was disappointing. They had not encountered any Shoshone. It was Sacagawea who gave them hope. Lewis wrote, "The Indian woman recognizes the country and assures us that this is the river on which her relations live, and that the three forks are at no great distance. This peice of information has cheered the sperits of the party, who now begin to console themselves with the anticipation of shortly seeing the head of the missouri, yet unknown to the civilized world."

THREE FORKS

Sacagawea promised that Three Forks of the Missouri were nearby. Clark set out to find them on July 23. He headed overland again with a small party consisting of Joseph and Reuben Field, Robert Frazer, and Charbonneau. They hiked 23 miles (37 km) that first day and 30 miles (48 km) the next. On the third day they reached the forks. Here, 2,464 miles (3,965 km) from its mouth on the Mississippi, the mighty Missouri divided into three clear and fast-running streams. It was a remarkably beautiful spot. Mountains were visible to the east, west, and south.

The westernmost fork of the Missouri was the largest. Clark believed that it led most directly to the mountains they sought. He noticed signs that American Indians had passed through the area within the past week. Clark left a message for Lewis attached to a pole. He then headed up the western fork to see what he could learn about the river's course.

Lewis arrived with the remainder of the party at the Three Forks two days later. Sacagawea was with him. She had now traveled back to the place of her kidnapping five years before by the Hidatsa. Lewis watched Sacagawea curiously. He wanted to see how she would react to finding herself again on home territory. He was surprised at her apparent indifference. "I cannot discover that she shews any immotion of sorrow in recollecting this event," he wrote, "or of joy in being again restored to her native country; if she has enough to eat and a few trinkets to wear I believe she would be perfectly content anywhere." Sacagawea had been through a lot in her young life. Displays of emotion had rarely won her any advantage. It is not surprising that, if she felt any great happiness at being back at Three Forks, she kept those feelings to herself.

Clark and his men rejoined the main party on the afternoon of July 27. The captains decided they should remain there for two days. The team needed to recuperate from the heavy exertions of recent weeks. They named the "three noble streams" that diverged at Three Forks after their country's leaders. The westernmost—and from their perspective, most important—branch was called the Jefferson. The middle branch was named the Madison, for Secretary of State James Madison. They called easternmost branch the Gallatin, for Secretary of the Treasury Albert Gallatin.

SEARCHING FOR THE SHOSHONE

In their homes back east, in Virginia and Kentucky, late July was the height of summer. In western Montana, however, it was a time when winter's approach could first be detected in the air. The days were hot. The nights were getting cold. Game was beginning to get scarce as well. Lewis began to worry, because they still had not met with the Shoshone. He wrote that "we begin to feel considerable anxiety with rispect to the Snake [Shoshone] Indians. if we do not find them or some other nation who have horses I fear the successfull issue of our voyage will be very doubtfull. . . ."

There was nothing to do but press on. They hoped that the next day or the next bend in the river would finally lead them to the Shoshone. On July 30, the Corps of Discovery set out up the Jefferson River. Clark was in a dugout canoe, and Lewis was on foot. He walked along the riverbank with Charbonneau and his wife. Sacagawea pointed out to Lewis the spot from which she had been kidnapped five years earlier.

Still no Shoshone, and the canoes were making slow progress. The river was no longer really navigable. The men often had to wade upstream dragging the canoes over the stony river bottom. Lewis decided to push on ahead overland. On August 1, he set out with Drouillard, Charbonneau, and Gass. On August 4, they came to another fork in the river. This time Lewis judged that the left, or east, fork was the one that came down most directly from the mountains. This fork would later become known as the Beaverhead River. Lewis left a note on a pole for Clark telling him to follow the left fork.

To make sure he had chosen correctly, however, Lewis decided to explore the right, or west, fork. When Clark reached the forks, he found no note from Lewis. A beaver had chewed down the pole on which it had been posted. So Clark followed Lewis's tracks up the right fork. Eventually, everything got straightened out. On August 7, the reunited party headed up the Beaverhead.

On August 8, they came to another significant landmark. A broad rock formation jutted up from the level valley plain. Lewis wrote,

> *The Indian woman recognized the point of a high plain . . . which she informed us was not very far from the summer retreat of her nation on a river beyond the mountains which runs to the west. This hill she says her nation calls the beaver's head. . . . She assures us that we shall either find her people on this river or on the river immediately west of it's source; which from its present size cannot be very distant.*

The next day, August 9, Lewis again headed off overland ahead of the main party. He took Drouillard, Shields, and McNeal as his companions. The following day they came to another fork in the Beaverhead. This time, Lewis decided it was no longer possible to travel by water. Here they would have to leave their canoes. Lewis wrote a note to

Clark. He asked Clark to halt at this spot and wait for his return. Lewis attached the note to a dry willow pole. He surely hoped that this time no beaver would gnaw it down. Meanwhile he was determined to press up the western branch of the divided stream (present-day Horse Prairie Creek), in search of the Shoshone.

On August 11, Lewis and the men set out up the west fork of the stream. Lewis had the men walk in a spread-out formation. This way they covered a distance of several hundred yards. They walked about five miles in this fashion, searching for signs of Shoshone. Lewis suddenly spotted a man on horseback. He was about two miles away across the plain and headed in their direction. Lewis studied the rider through his telescope. The man's clothing was unlike any that Lewis had seen before on an American Indian. He concluded this must be a Shoshone. "I was overjoyed at the sight of this stranger," Lewis wrote, "and had no doubt of obtaining a friendly introduction to his nation provided I could get near enough to him to convince him of our being whitemen."

When he was about a mile from Lewis, the native halted. Lewis took a blanket from his pack. He held two corners, threw it up into the air, and then brought it close to the ground as if spreading it out. He repeated this gesture three times. This gesture, Lewis had been told by other tribes, was a sign of peaceful intentions. The horseman was still wary. Leaving his rifle behind, Lewis advanced alone. As he walked, he rolled up his sleeve to show off his white skin. He held out trade trinkets in his hand. When he was close enough to be heard by the rider, he called out the word *tab-ba-bone*. Sacagawea had told him this was the Shoshone word for "white man." The word actually meant "stranger." The Shoshone Indians actually had no word for white man since they had never met one.

The rider let Lewis get within about 100 paces. Then he suddenly turned his horse, whipped him into a gallop, and rode off out of sight. There would be no meeting with the Shoshone that day, but they now knew that the Shoshone were close by. They pressed on eagerly toward the mountains. Lewis fixed a small American flag to a pole. When they came in sight of another native, he would display it as a signal of their peaceable intentions. (Lewis never explained why he thought the Shoshone would recognize or respond favorably to the American flag.)

On August 12, 1805, Lewis and three other members of the Corps of Discovery crossed the Continental Divide at Lemhi Pass, a two-mile (three-kilometer) span in the Rocky Mountains on the border between present-day Montana and Idaho. As the first Americans to cross the boundary of the Louisiana Purchase, the men officially left the United States and entered foreign territory.

The next day, August 12, 1805, Lewis sent George Drouillard to look for the trail of the American Indian they had spotted the day before. It was still early morning when Drouillard returned. He did not find the American Indian's trail. Still Lewis decided to press on up a high wooded hillside. There, the stream they had camped along branched into smaller brooks. As always, Lewis kept his eyes open for unfamiliar plant and animal life to write about in his journal. The men saw signs of American Indian presence. People searching for edible roots had dug up the ground by the stream.

They found an Indian path that led into the mountains. The path became steeper, but they pushed on, their excitement mounting. "[T]he road was still plain," Lewis wrote in his journal. "I therefore did not dispair of shortly finding a passage over the mountains and of taisting the waters of the great Columbia this evening." Up and up they walked until finally they came to the spring that fed the little brook they walked alongside. This, Lewis believed, was the headwater of the mighty Missouri River. His joy knew no bounds: "I had accomplished one of those great objects on which my mind has been unalterably fixed for many years."

It was another half-mile to the mountain's summit. The pass ahead, later named Lemhi Pass, crossed the Continental Divide. No non-American Indian had ever before stepped across the Continental Divide. Here, on the eastern side of the mountains, all waters flowed east or southward, to the Mississippi River and the Gulf of Mexico. On the western side, all waters flowed to the Pacific. Lewis fully expected to find the headwaters of the Columbia River on the far slope. However, there was no sign of the Columbia River and the easy water route that he had dreamed of finding. Instead, as Lewis wrote, "I discovered immence ranges of high mountains still to the West of us with their tops partially covered with snow." The corps had a long, hard way to go before they would see the Pacific Ocean.

6

To the Pacific

CAPTAIN LEWIS AND HIS MEN REACHED THE CONTINENTAL DIVIDE
on August 12, 1805. The men did not linger long atop the mountain.
They still had to find the Shoshone. They camped that night on the
western slope. When they went to sleep, they were spending their
first night on foreign territory. Having stepped over the Continental
Divide, they had also crossed the bounds of the Louisiana Purchase.
They had entered a region that was, as yet, the property of none
of the "Great White Fathers" in Washington or London. Here, the
American Indian tribes remained independent and sovereign. Those
American Indians were going to be very important to determining
the success or failure of the Lewis and Clark expedition in the months
to come.

MEETING THE SHOSHONE

They set off early the next morning. They soon spotted a group of American
Indians about a mile away from them, including a man, two women,
and their dogs. The American Indians saw them as well. Lewis put down
his rifle and unfurled the American flag. He shouted, "tab-ba-bone."

The results of his greeting were the same as the last encounter. The
flag did not reassure the American Indians. They took one look at these
self-proclaimed *tab-ba-bone* and fled. Only the dogs lingered. Lewis
tried to tie some trade goods around the neck of one of the animals in
a handkerchief. He thought this would "persuade [the Shoshone] of our
pacific disposition toward them." They too fled.

Lewis and the men followed the path the American Indians had taken. After about a mile, they spied another group of American Indians. There was one elderly woman, one young woman, and a girl of about 12 years of age. The young woman ran off. The old woman and the girl remained seated on the ground. They probably believed they would be captured or killed.

Lewis tried to reassure the women that he meant them no harm. His face and hands were tanned by the sun "quite as dark as their own." So he rolled up his sleeve to show his white skin. He pressed some trinkets into their hands and repeated "tab-ba-bone." The old woman called to the younger woman who had fled to come back. Lewis dipped his finger in some of the red paint he was carrying. He painted the cheeks of the women. This gesture was a sign of peace among the American Indians. Using sign language, he asked them to lead his party to their chief.

Just two miles farther down the path, they met a band of 60 warriors. The men were on horseback. They were probably alerted by the first group that had fled from Lewis. The American Indians were armed for battle. Coolly and courageously, Lewis advanced toward the riders. He was unarmed, carrying the flag on its pole. One can only imagine the absolute amazement these Shoshone warriors must have felt. Here was a strange man in a cocked hat holding his piece of red, white, and blue cloth dangling from a stick. The Shoshone women called out that these strangers came bearing gifts and meant no harm. Instantly, the war party became a welcoming party. The chief and other warriors dismounted. They rushed to hug Lewis and his men, saying in their own language "I am much pleased." Lewis was, of course, equally happy. He was somewhat less happy that they were so demonstrative of their feelings. "We were all carresed and besmeared with their grease and paint till I was heartily tired of the national hug." The Corps of Discovery had met the Shoshone at last.

Lewis and his men sat in a circle on the ground with the chief, Cameahwait. The chief's name means "The One Who Never Walks." Lewis handed out more trinkets. He gave Cameahwait the American flag he had been carrying when they met. "I informed him [the flag] was an emblem of peace among whitemen." After smoking a ceremonial pipe, they followed Cameahwait and his men to the tribe's camp.

Cameahwait's people were the Lemhi Shoshone band. They were part of the Northern Shoshone tribe of the Rocky Mountains. Lewis and Clark knew them as the Snake Indians. Part of the year, from May to September, they lived in their preferred setting, the Lemhi River valley west of the Continental Divide. There they fished. During the rest of the year they hunted buffalo on the plains east of the divide. They did not look forward to this hunting trip. It held constant danger from raiding parties of Hidatsa, Blackfeet, and other tribes. As soon as they had enough buffalo meat to last through the winter, they returned to the mountains. When Lewis arrived at their camp, they were getting ready to make their journey to the plains.

In need of horses, Lewis and his men looked for Shoshone with whom they could trade. The warriors were suspicious of their intentions, but finally became convinced that the men came in peace. These were the first white men the Shoshone had ever seen.

The Shoshone had never met white men. Lewis and his men believed them to be a poor tribe, especially when compared to tribes such as the Mandan. The Shoshone, however, were rich in one important resource. Cameahwait owned a herd of about 400 horses. Lewis knew a thing or two about horse breeding. He wrote that he would have been proud to ride some of the Shoshone horses "on the South side of James River" in his home state of Virginia.

There was more ceremonial smoking of tobacco and exchanges of presents at the riverside camp. The Shoshone fed the white men from their own meager food supplies. They ate dried fruit cakes. Lewis was offered a small piece of roasted fish. Its taste pleased him immensely. "This was the first salmon I had seen and perfectly convinced me that we were on the waters of the Pacific Ocean."

RETURN TO LEMHI PASS

Lewis explained to Cameahwait that there was "another Chief and a large party of whitemen" coming up the river on the other side of the mountain. He explained that they wanted to trade for horses with Cameahwait's people; Lewis promised to send many more white men to come with trading goods.

The promise of future trade pleased Cameahwait. The Shoshone desperately needed muskets to defend themselves against hostile tribes. He agreed to return with Lewis to meet up with Clark and the rest of the expedition. However, the Shoshone soon lost their enthusiasm for the arrangement. Perhaps they suspected some kind of trick. How could they be sure these white strangers were not working with their enemies? Eventually Lewis shamed Cameahwait into keeping his word. "I still hoped that there were some among them who were not affraid to die, that there were men [who] would go with me and convince themselves of the truth of what I had asscerted." Cameahwait would allow no one doubt his bravery. He once again agreed to go with Lewis. When Cameahwait and a group of warriors left for Lemhi Pass, the old women of the tribe wept. They feared they would never see their men again. Lewis, Cameahwait, and the others had not gone far before a whole crowd of villagers decided to join them.

The Shoshone still feared treachery. They gave Lewis and his men Shoshone headwear to wear. If an ambush lay ahead, the white men would be targets too. Lewis voluntarily gave Cameahwait his gun. He told Cameahwait in sign language that he could shoot him if they were attacked.

They eventually reached the forks of the Beaverhead. Unfortunately, Clark and his party had not yet arrived. Thinking fast, Lewis had Drouillard fetch a note that he left at the campsite for Clark a few days earlier. Lewis told Cameahwait it was a message from Clark saying that he would arrive the next day with the main party. The Shoshone were suspicious. They complained that they were "told different stories."

Lewis tried to keep the Shoshone interested. He told them that there was a woman of their own tribe traveling with Clark. He added "we had a man with us who was black and had short curling hair." This astonished the Shoshone. Lewis concluded that "they seemed quite as anxious to see this monster," meaning York, "as they wer the merchandise which we had to barter for their horses." Lewis slept uneasily that night. He feared that the Shoshone would slip back across the mountain to safety. If they did, the expedition would be doomed.

A DAY OF REUNIONS

Early the next morning, August 17, Drouillard and several Shoshone set out to find Clark and the rest of the corps. They soon found them. Sacagawea was one of the first to see Drouillard and his Shoshone companions. According to Clark she "danced for the joyful Sight." She recognized the American Indians as her own people. Clark's party soon reached Lewis. Cameahwait greeted the new white chief warmly. He tied small pieces of seashell into Clark's hair in greeting. Sacagawea recognized another woman who had been captured with her. Unlike Sacagawea, the woman had managed to escape her captors.

Then came the most unexpected reunion of all. Lewis and Clark sat down with Cameahwait to negotiate. Sacagawea and Charbonneau were called over to translate. Sacagawea suddenly recognized Cameahwait as her own long-lost brother. Weeping with joy, she ran to Cameahwait and hugged him. There was no longer any doubt that the Shoshone would help the white strangers. Lewis and Clark named the meeting place at the forks of the Beaverhead River "Camp Fortunate."

Everyone seemed to have a very good time. The Shoshone were impressed by Lewis's air gun, by his dog, Seaman, and by York. They saw for themselves that he was a man, not a monster. Lewis bought a few horses. He paid with items from the expedition's collection of trade goods.

August 18 was Lewis's birthday. He was depressed. Perhaps he was feeling a long way from home, with a long way still to go to reach the Pacific. That day Lewis wrote about his feelings in his journal. "This day I completed my thirty-first year . . . I reflected that I had as yet done but little, very little, indeed, to further the hapiness of the human race or to advance the information of the succeeding generation." He regretted the time he had wasted in his youth. He should have improved himself and learned more. He resolved "in future, to live for mankind, as I have heretofore lived for myself." Perhaps this resolution made Lewis feel better, perhaps not. A little over a week later he stopped making daily journal entries. With rare exceptions, he did not resume until January 1 of the following year.

ROUTE-FINDING

That same morning Clark set out with Cameahwait. Most of the Shoshone, 11 men from the corps, and Sacagawea joined them. Cameahwait warned Lewis that the rivers west of the Continental Divide were difficult to navigate. The white men took axes with them anyway to build canoes in case Clark could find a water route.

Lewis stayed behind with the rest of the Corps of Discovery. They waited for Cameahwait to return with the horses. In the meantime, they prepared a cache for supplies. They sank the dugouts with stones in a nearby pond, keeping them safe for future use. They built wooden packsaddles to carry supplies.

Clark asked Cameahwait about the path that lay ahead of the expedition. Until this time they had followed directions given the previous winter by the Hidatsa. The Hidatsa knew little of the land to the west of the Rockies. Lewis and Clark had expected to find the "southern fork" of the Columbia when they crossed the Continental Divide. They now were coming to understand that there was no southern fork of the Columbia. Could they travel by tributary streams to the Columbia? If so, they could still fulfill President Jefferson's dream of finding a mostly water-borne passageway across the continent.

The Lemhi River intersected another larger river (the present-day Salmon) a few miles to the north. The Salmon headed north. Then its main fork headed westward. This was the direction they wanted to go. Cameahwait warned Clark that the fast-running Salmon cut through a deep canyon with impassable slopes. It would not suit their purpose.

There was another route, Cameahwait told Clark. Unfortunately, it involved a long overland trek. They could follow the banks of the Salmon River's north fork. Then they could hike a rough trail through steep hills into another river valley. Eventually they would find a westward trail. It led to a pass through even higher mountains than they had already encountered. American Indians used this trail regularly. These were the "persed [pierced] nosed Indians." They lived on a river that "ran a great way toward the seting sun and finally lost itself in a great lake of water which was illy taisted and where the white men lived."

The description of the ill-tasting great lake sounded to Clark like the Pacific. If American Indians could take the trail across the western mountains, he believed white men could as well. Cameahwait's words "instantly settled" for Clark the route the expedition should take. The hope of a water route to the Pacific finally died.

Cameahwait headed back across Lemhi Pass to join Lewis at Camp Fortunate. Sacagawea, Charbonneau, and about 50 Shoshone joined him. They did more horse trading. They finally loaded supplies on the newly made packsaddles and headed over the pass on August 24.

Cameahwait wanted to please his new white friends. They had been good to his sister. They had also promised to bring trade goods and guns to the Shoshone. However, there was a problem. The whites wanted the Shoshone to stay camped along the Lemhi River while they purchased more horses from them. Cameahwait's people were running out of food. They needed to come east to the buffalo plains as soon as possible. Cameahwait secretly sent some of his men out on the morning of August 25. They alerted the rest of his band that it was time to break camp and move east.

Sacagawea now showed how loyal she was to the Americans. She learned of Cameahwait's secret plan and told Charbonneau. Her husband did not seem to think it was important news. He finally mentioned it to Lewis several hours later. "I was out of patience with the folly of Charbono," Lewis fumed in a journal entry. If the Shoshone headed east, then they could not trade with them for more horses. This would be a disaster for the expedition.

Lewis confronted Cameahwait. He once again threatened and shamed the Shoshone chief. If Cameahwait led his people east, Lewis promised that no whites would ever trade arms to the Shoshone. Eventually the chief agreed to tell his people to remain in their camp. The expedition was saved. Lewis unfortunately did not fully appreciate the sacrifice that the Shoshone were making on behalf of the self-righteous white strangers.

Lewis and his men reached the Shoshone camp on August 26. That night there was fiddle music and dancing. The partying was "much to the amusement and gratification of the American Indians." Cameahwait promised that they would trade for horses the next day. Lewis spent another uneasy night fearing "that the caprice of the indians might suddenly induce them to withhold their horses from us . . ."

Lewis got his horses. He did not, however, get the ones he had admired earlier. The Shoshone made the white men pay a high price in their trade goods for a collection of old and ailing nags. These were not at all the kind of animals that Lewis would have chosen to ride back home in Virginia. There was nothing to be done about it. They needed mounts, and now they had them.

Clark rejoined Lewis on August 29. They left the following day, guided by a Shoshone named Old Toby and his son. The group set out overland up the Lemhi River and then up the north fork of the Salmon River. They slogged through ankle-deep snow. The rough terrain reminded them to move as fast as they could before the onset of winter.

SALISH COUNTRY

A few days later, the Corps of Discovery left the banks of the Salmon River. They crossed over what later became known as Lost Trail Pass and entered the Bitterroot Valley. There they met another tribe of American Indians, the Salish tribe. "[T]hose people recved us friendly," Clark wrote in his journal, "threw white robes [over] our Sholders & Smoked in the pipes of peace."

This photograph taken by Edward Curtis in about 1910 shows four Salish (Flathead) women sitting on the ground preparing meat, probably the same way it had been done at the time of Lewis and Clark. The Corps of Discovery encountered about 400 Salish Indians, 40 lodges, and nearly 500 horses. The Salish generously traded their fresh horses for the broken-down ones in the expedition's herd.

Lewis and Clark bought more horses from the Salish. The Salish generously exchanged some of their fresh mounts for the broken-down Shoshone cast-offs. Now with about 40 horses, they could lighten the packs each animal carried. This helped them make good time as they headed north alongside the Bitterroot River. Lining the broad river valley on both sides were mountain ranges. To the east were the relatively gentle Sapphire Mountains. To the west were the higher, more jagged, and increasingly snow-covered Bitterroot Mountains. This was the direction they were headed. Under other circumstances the scenery might have inspired them, but their stomachs were empty and they did not care. On September 6, Clark noted bleakly that there was "nothing to eat but berries, our flour out, and but little Corn, the hunters killed 2 pheasents only . . ." Several days of hard rain did nothing to lift their spirits.

THE HARDEST STRETCH

On September 9, the Corps of Discovery camped on a "fine bould clear running stream." They were about 10 miles (16 km) south of present-day Missoula, Montana. They called this stream Traveler's Rest Creek. Old Toby gave them news there that was both encouraging and discouraging. To the east lay a trail alongside a river (present-day Big Blackfoot River). On their return trip, they could follow that trail over an easy pass through the mountains. In just four days they would reach the Missouri River near the Great Falls. The previous winter the Hidatsa had tried to tell them about this pass, but they had misunderstood the directions. As a result, they had wasted nearly two months traveling south to the headwaters of the Missouri.

Meanwhile, they still had to cross the high Bitterroot Mountains to the west. The men did not look forward to what lay ahead. "The snow makes them look like the middle of winter," Joseph Whitehouse wrote in his journal. They were "the most terrible mountains that I ever beheld," according to Sergeant Gass.

On September 11, the expedition began its struggle across the Bitterroots. Horses slipped on the steep footing and rolled down the hillsides, scattering the supplies. No one was killed or injured. This seems a miracle. The phrase "much fatigued" appeared day after day in Clark's journal. Bad weather added to their woes. Eight inches of snow fell on September 16. Clark wrote, "I have been as wet and as cold in every part as I ever was in my life."

The names they gave to places along the trail are evidence of their days of hunger. There was "Killed Colt Creek" where they stopped to eat one of the colts in their herd. At "Hungery Creek" they failed to have even that poor a meal. In their 11 days in the Bitterroots, they managed to kill only five deer. This was just slightly more than a single day's ration of four deer. The howling coyotes did not make for restful nights. When Captain Lewis killed one, it went into the pot to feed the men.

NEZ PERCE HOSPITALITY

On September 18, Clark set off with six men. They were in search of open country and better hunting. Two days later, they reached the Weippe Prairie in present-day Clearwater County, Idaho. There they came across a group of Nez Perce Indians. The Nez Perce directed them to another settlement on the Clearwater River. A chief named Twisted Hair led this group.

Like the Shoshone, most of the Nez Perce had never encountered white men. The tribe debated what to do about the strangers. Some thought they should kill them and take their rifles. An old woman named Watkuweis was the only Nez Perce who had ever seen whites before. Like Sacagawea, a rival tribe had captured her. Fortunately her experience with whites had been good. "These are the people who helped me," she said of the whites. "Do them no hurt."

The Nez Perce fed the famished white strangers on dried salmon and bread made from camas roots. Clark and his men ate heartily. Unfortunately the food did not sit well in their empty stomachs. "I find myself verry unwell all the evening," Clark wrote, "from eating the fish & roots too freely." The next day was no better. "I am very sick today," Clark wrote, "and puke which relive me." Lewis and the rest of the party stumbled down out of the Bitterroot Range on September 22. Clark unsuccessfully tried to warn them to go easy on the salmon and camas roots. They stuffed themselves, as starving people will. Soon they were as sick as Clark and his men.

Despite their illness, Lewis and Clark carried out their duties. They handed out Jefferson medals to Twisted Hair and several other chiefs. Twisted Hair drew them a map on a piece of white elk skin. The map showed how to travel by lesser rivers westward to the Columbia River. He and another chief named Tetoharsky agreed to accompany Lewis and Clark through Nez Perce territory as far as the Columbia.

On September 26, Clark established the "Canoe Camp" on a site five miles west of present-day Orofino, Idaho. Virtually all the Corps of Discovery were still sick. With the help of the Nez Perce, they soon built five dugout canoes. The Nez Perce showed them how to burn out the interior of felled trees to save labor. By October 6, their new fleet was complete. They branded their remaining horses. Then they turned them over to the temporary care of the Nez Perce.

THE NEZ PERCE HORSES

Spanish explorers introduced horses to the North American continent in the mid-sixteenth century. No other European import had as dramatic an impact on the lives of Western Indians. When the Western Indians acquired horses, they swiftly changed long-established patterns of settlement, warfare, hunting, and trading.

The Nez Perce first acquired horses around 1700. They used their horses for transportation. Each year whole villages would migrate from the valleys of the Columbia, Snake, and Clearwater rivers to lands close to the Rockies. There they gathered camas roots and fruit, hunted, and fished the mountain streams.

The Nez Perce were known as expert horse breeders. Appaloosa horses, with their distinctive spotted coats, were often to be found in Nez Perce herds. The Nez Perce valued their horses highly. They painted their coats and decorated their halters and saddles with beads, dye, and porcupine quills.

On the afternoon of October 7, the Corps of Discovery proceeded on down the Clearwater River in their new dugout canoes. Two months earlier they had expected a short portage connecting the waters of the Missouri to the waters of the Columbia. Instead they had experienced a difficult journey over 400 miles (643 km) of rugged terrain. It must have been a great relief to find themselves once again riding in canoes. Even better, they were traveling with the current, instead of against it as they had all the long way up the Missouri River. The Clearwater River was flowing toward the Pacific.

DOWN THE CLEARWATER AND THE SNAKE

The dangers of the Clearwater were not to be underestimated. On the expedition's day on the river, one of the canoes struck a rock and sprung a leak. Fortunately, it remained afloat. The men were able to repair it that night. Despite the accident, the corps traveled 20 miles (32 km) that day. After making a further 18 miles (29 km) the next day, another canoe struck a tree top. It filled rapidly and overturned. The men and supplies it carried were dumped in the rapids. The expedition stopped on a nearby island to dry their goods and make repairs.

On October 10, the explorers set off again down the Clearwater. Despite yet another near-disastrous encounter between a canoe and a rock, they covered an extraordinary 60 miles (9,656 km) of river that day. This was the farthest they had ever come in a single day. They were now in present-day Washington State. That night they slept at the site where the Clearwater and the Snake rivers flow together.

The corps continued westward along the Snake River. The landscape changed dramatically. The country around them now contained rolling hills and canyons. The ponderosa pines that lined the shores of the Clearwater disappeared. There was now "no timber of any kind," Clark noted.

In five days on the Snake, they traveled less than 120 miles (193 km). The journey down the Snake was full of hazards. They had hired three American Indian guides to help navigate the Snake's rapids. Even the guides could not prevent the canoes' frequent spills. These mishaps cost them irreplaceable supplies and valuable time. A dugout piloted by Drouillard struck a rock on October 14 and sank. They lost blankets, tomahawks, shot pouches, and other goods.

ON TO THE COLUMBIA

On October 16, they reached the Columbia River. The Corps of Discovery's arrival at the Columbia rivaled the crossing of the Continental Divide in its importance. Jefferson's soldiers had found a route linking the major river crossing the plains with the major river that flowed to the Pacific.

When they reached the Columbia, Lewis and Clark were back on a river that had already been explored by white men. Men had already journeyed about 100 (160 km) miles up the river from the Pacific. They were thus linked again to the world they had known in the East.

Lewis and Clark found new reasons to be glad they had brought Sacagawea along. On October 13, Clark wrote, "The wife of Shabono our interpetr we find reconsiles all the Indians, as to our friendly intentions—a woman with a party of men is a token of peace." The two Nez

Perce chiefs, Twisted Hair and Tetoharsky, also served as a sign that the white men were not to be feared or attacked. They set off ahead of the expedition. As they came to native settlements, they announced the arrival of the corps. The tribes in this region were related to the Nez Perce. They spoke dialects of the same language, known to later generations of linguists as Sahaptian.

Twisted Hair and Tetoharsky's advance work helped win a particularly friendly reception for the Corps of Discovery when they first arrived at the Columbia. The Yakama and Wanapam Indians were camped there, drying fish and repairing their gear at the end of the annual salmon run. Clark recorded that the local chief came to see them "at the head of about 200 men Singing and beeting on their drums . . ." The Yakama and Wanapam formed a half circle around the white men "and Sung for Some time . . ."

Lewis and Clark spent two days with the Yakama and Wanapam. The explorers received maps of the Columbia from the chiefs. They also learned about the tribes they might meet along their route. On October 18, the corps set sail down the last river they would follow to the Pacific. Sergeant Gass recorded in his journal entry for the day that "we proceeded down the Great Columbia, which is a very beautiful river."

On their first day on the Columbia they met the Walla Walla tribe. The chief, Yellepit, gave them another friendly reception. Yellepit brought the whites a basket of berries as a gift. In turn, he received one of the Jefferson medals. The chief wanted Lewis and Clark to stay for a while. The captains, however, were worried about the approach of winter. They promised to stay longer with the Walla Walla on their return trip.

DIFFICULT WATERS

The Corps of Discovery at first enjoyed smooth sailing on the Columbia. This soon changed. On October 22, the expedition came to what Lewis and Clark called the Great Falls of the Columbia. They were later renamed Celilo Falls. Here the river's elevation drops 38.5 feet (11.7 m) in a series of falls and cataracts. The river also narrowed at the falls. It was an excellent spot for fishing. For 10,000 years, Celilo Falls had attracted American Indians to the area. It was one of the longest-settled communities in North America. To Lewis and Clark, however, it was just an obstacle. To get past the falls, they portaged their supplies along a narrow trail.

They soon met another challenge. On October 24, the river narrowed again. Clark described this passage of the river as an "agitated gut swelling, boiling & whorling in every direction." The corps had to get through two sets of difficult rapids. They considered another portage, but decided it would take too much time. Instead, they ran the canoes down the narrows. The American Indians watched from the riverbanks. Clearly they expected the foolish white men to drown in the attempt. Luckily, the corps passed the narrows without mishap.

The river was changing. So were the peoples who lived along it. This section of riverbank functioned as a center of trade. It drew from many tribes. It also served as a linguistic and cultural dividing line. To the west, the tribes spoke Sahaptian languages. To the east, they spoke Chinookan languages. The Sahaptian- and Chinookan-speaking tribes were enemies. Twisted Hair and Tetoharsky knew that if they went any further they would be in hostile territory. For several days they had been asking to turn back and go home. Lewis and Clark persuaded them to stay with the expedition. They wanted to try to broker peace between the tribes. The Nez Perce chiefs agreed.

Lewis and Clark held a peace council on the evening of October 24. A chief from the Wishram-Wasco band of Chinookan-speaking people came to their camp. The men smoked pipes. Lewis and Clark handed out medals. Then they urged the tribes of the lower and upper Columbia to put aside their weapons. "[W]e have every reason to believe," Clark wrote, "that those two bands of nations are and will be on the most friendly terms with each other." This was wishful thinking. Twisted Hair and Tetoharsky headed home the next day. They remained anxious to return to the safety of Sahaptian-speaking territory. The Corps of Discovery was once again on its own.

THE WESTERN COLUMBIA

The corps soon met another narrow, dangerous stretch of river. The captains decided to portage their goods and dugouts rather than push their luck any further. On October 31, they found a "remarkable high detached rock" on the north shore of the Columbia. This volcanic stone is almost 900 feet (274 m) in height. Lewis and Clark named it Beacon Rock.

They were still more than 100 miles (160 km) from the ocean. They began to feel the effects of the tides on the river. The river water began to taste salty. Soon they would have to rely on rainwater to drink. Luckily, there was no shortage of rainwater. The mountains they were now passing on either side of the river worked a dramatic change in the climate.

The expedition soon reached the mouth of a river entering the southern side of the Columbia, the present-day Sandy River. This was the highest point on the Columbia River ever reached by explorers traveling west from the Pacific. Thus, for the first time since April, they were back in territory previously visited by whites.

In the early 1800s, the Columbia River provided one of the few open paths through the Cascade Range. Later this path was known as the Columbia Gorge. The Cascades stretch from present-day northern California through Oregon and Washington. This volcanic ridge averages 5,000 feet (1,524 m) in height. It is dotted with peaks that reach twice that height or more. Moving west through the Columbia Gorge, the Corps of Discovery entered a region of deep forests. East of the Cascades, annual rainfall is limited to about six inches. West of the Cascades, 10 times as much falls every year. Rain clouds roll in from the Pacific, bump up against the mountains, and go no further.

The explorers were in a hurry to get to the ocean. They never spent more than one night with the local Chinook Indians. White men were no novelty to the Chinook. The corps saw one native wearing a sailor's jacket. Others had iron pots, brass teakettles, and muskets. They even began hearing a few words of spoken English. Lewis recorded hearing "musquit, powder, shot, knife, [and] file. . ." The Chinook knew the value of goods, especially food. "They asc high prices for what they Sell," Clark complained.

AT LAST THE PACIFIC

On November 7, Lewis and Clark knew the Pacific could not be far off. That afternoon, they could see the river widen dramatically. They could hear the sound of waves crashing on the shore ahead. Clark made no attempt to disguise his emotions. He recorded the most famous sentence he would ever write, "Ocian in view! O! the joy."

Unfortunately, Clark was wrong. The waves were genuine. However, they were crashing in Gray's Bay, part of the Columbia estuary, not the

Route of Lewis and Clark's Corps of Discovery, August 12–November 7, 1805

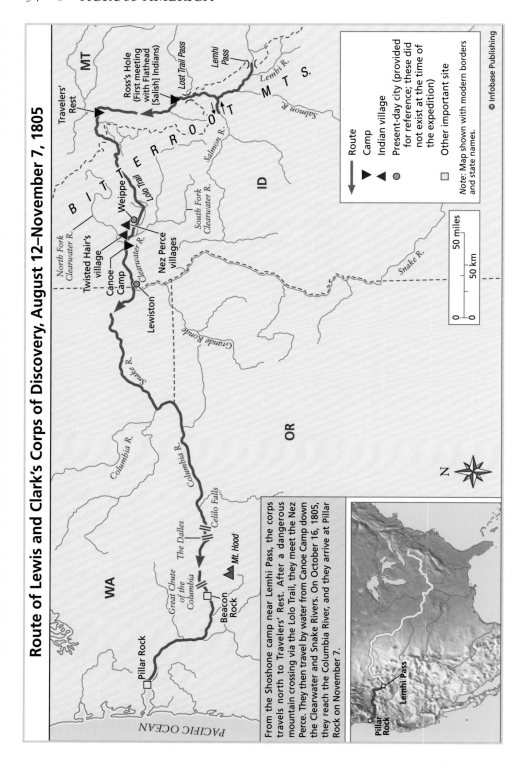

From the Shoshone camp near Lemhi Pass, the corps travels north to Travelers' Rest. After a dangerous mountain crossing via the Lolo Trail, they meet the Nez Perce. They then travel by water from Canoe Camp down the Clearwater and Snake Rivers. On October 16, 1805, they reach the Columbia River, and they arrive at Pillar Rock on November 7.

© Infobase Publishing

Route

Camp

Indian village

Present-day city (provided for reference; these did not exist at the time of the expedition)

Other important site

Note: Map shown with modern borders and state names.

N

0   50 miles
0   50 km

edge of the Pacific. They were still 20 miles (32 km) from the ocean. They would not prove to be an easy 20 miles.

The Pacific Northwest winter was settling in. It was the worst time to be navigating the Columbia estuary in clumsy dugout canoes. Driving rain and high waves cut short their river travel on November 8. "The Canoes roled in Such a manner as to cause Several [expedition members] to be verry Sick," Clark reported. For two miserable days they camped on the northern side of Gray's Bay. There was a lull in the storm on November 10. This let them gain an additional eight miles (12 km) down the river, to Point Ellice, near present-day Meglar, Washington. There they were trapped again by bad weather for several more days. Everything was wet. No one could sleep. They were cold, exhausted, and hungry.

Clark described this time as "the most disagreeable time I have experienced." Finally, on the afternoon of November 15, the rain briefly stopped. They were able to sail down to Chinook Point. They were finally in sight of the ocean. There they camped for the next nine days. Lewis and a small group hiked to the end of Cape Disappointment. Lewis carved his initials in a tree. Then he walked along the ocean beach. Clark visited the ocean with another party a few days later. The "men appear much Satisfied with their trip beholding with estonishment the high waves dashing against the rocks & this emence ocian," he wrote on November 18. On November 19, Clark's party walked about nine miles (14 km) up the coast, to about the site of present-day Long Beach, Washington. There, he too carved his name and the date on a small pine tree.

They were at the end of their journey to the Pacific. Back in the winter of 1803–1804, Clark estimated the distance they would have to travel. His estimates had proven reasonably accurate as they explored the Lower Missouri. However his estimate of the distance from the Mandan village to the Pacific of was off by 1,000 miles (1,609 km). They had traveled roughly 2,550 (4,103 km) miles between April and November 1805. All together they had come 4,142 miles (6,665 km) from the mouth of the Missouri to the mouth of the Columbia.

Some members of the Corps of Discovery wanted to head back up the Columbia for a drier climate. Lewis and Clark disagreed. They feared it would be much colder inland. The Clatsop Indians who lived on the southern shore of the river had told them that elk were abundant in nearby woods. If they stayed close to the ocean, they could hunt elk to eat during the winter. They could use the elk skins to make new clothing and moccasins. They could also make salt from the ocean water. The salt would preserve and flavor their food. Another benefit of staying by the ocean was the possibility of meeting an American or British merchant ship. This would allow them to purchase supplies. The ship might even carry a copy of their journals back to Jefferson.

Lewis and Clark put the question to a vote on November 24. After some debate, the proposal to seek a winter campsite near the ocean got the most votes. All of the men were allowed to participate in the vote, including Clark's slave, York. Sacagawea's preference was noted. However, her vote was not counted in Clark's final tally.

FORT CLATSOP

They crossed to the south bank of the Columbia on November 26. Lewis took a party inland. He found a spot for a winter camp in the forest near a freshwater spring. The spot was three miles up a small river that is now known as the Lewis and Clark River. They moved to the site on December 7 and started building their third and final winter camp. They named it Fort Clatsop after the local tribe.

The new fort enclosed an area about 50 square feet (15 sq. m). Two long barracks rows faced each other across a small parade ground. There were gates in both the front and back walls. The captains had a room to themselves in the barracks, as did Charbonneau and his family. The enlisted men bunked eight to a room. The fort was not designed for comfort. It provided a roof over their heads. They needed one. Of the 161 days they spent at Fort Clatsop, they enjoyed only 12 days without rain.

There were few diversions to break up the monotony of life that winter. One came on January 5. Local American Indians told them of a whale washed up on the beach a few miles away. Clark prepared to set out to find the whale. He hoped to obtain something to eat other than elk and salmon. He was also eager for an outing. Much to the captains' surprise, Sacagawea virtually demanded to come along. "The Indian woman was very impo[r]tunate to be permitted to go," Lewis wrote, "and was therefore indulged; she observed that she had traveled a long way with us to see the great waters, and that now that monstrous fish

Fort Clatsop was the last encampment before the Corps of Discovery began their return trip to St. Louis. The leaders selected the area where they would build the fort for several reasons: the elk was abundant, there was plenty of timber, the American Indians were friendly, and it was close to the Pacific Ocean and the Columbia River.

was also to be seen, she thought it very hard she could not be permitted to see either (she had never yet been to the Ocean)."

Sacagawea got her wish and saw the ocean. Of the "monstrous fish," there was not much left. The local Tillamook tribe had gotten there first. They had stripped off all the meat and blubber. The trip was not wasted, however. The group purchased 300 pounds of blubber and some whale oil from the Tillamook. The whale proved a welcome, if exotic, addition to their diet. It was entirely consumed by the end of January. We "prize it highly," Lewis wrote.

THOUGHTS OF HOME

Whenever they were in sight of the ocean, they looked for the sails of a merchant ship. None appeared. There would be no news from home and no opportunity to send copies of their journals to Jefferson by sea. Most critically, they would be unable to replenish their dwindling supply of trade goods. They now had only enough trade goods to fill two handkerchiefs. It was going to be a frugal trip back to St. Louis.

They made do with what they had at hand. There was game to be hunted and meat to be preserved. They turned elk skins into clothing and moccasins. These replaced the worn and rotting garments and footwear they had worn down the Columbia. In late December, some of the men set up a camp on the seacoast to make salt. They boiled saltwater in five large kettles. When the water boiled off, they scraped out the salt that was left over. Lewis pronounced the salt to be "excellent, fine, strong & white." He reported with gusto how much more he was enjoying his food now that it could be seasoned.

Clark devoted his time to mapmaking. He noted on February 14: "I have compleated a map of the Counterey through which we have been passing from the Mississippi at the Mouth of the Missouri to this place." The Corps of Discovery, he claimed optimistically, had succeeded in finding "the most practicable and navigable passage across the Continent of North America."

While Clark drew his maps, Lewis wrote in his journal. He wrote long entries describing the local plant and animal life. He also recorded observations of Chinookan customs, dress, and appearance. Lewis displayed his talents as an artist. The pages of his journal from that winter are filled with images. Today these images symbolize the discoveries of the Corps of Discovery.

The captains knew there was no point in heading east too soon. An early spring start would only bring them to a dead halt once they reached the snowbound Rockies. They could not cross the mountains before June, at the earliest. However, life at Fort Clatsop proved unbearable. They could no longer put up with the rain-soaked days and flea-bitten nights. They had originally planned to set off eastward on the Columbia on April 1. By early March, they had decided to leave as soon as possible.

There was one big problem. They no longer had enough canoes to carry everyone. Only three of their dugouts remained seaworthy. Lewis traded his uniform coat for one Indian canoe. They could not find another one available for a price they were willing to pay. So they decided to steal another canoe from the local Clatsop Indians. These were the people who had been very friendly to them throughout the winter. The theft of the Clatsop canoe was not the Corps of Discovery's finest moment.

By mid-March, they were packing the canoes. Then, typically, the weather turned bad. They waited impatiently through four days of steady rain. On March 22, Lewis vowed that the expedition would leave the next day "at all events." As it turned out, the weather finally cooperated. The rain stopped about midday on March 23. Wasting no time, the men hurriedly packed their belongings. At 1 P.M., they proceeded on up the Columbia. The Corps of Discovery was going home.

7

Homeward Bound

ANOTHER LONG WINTER CAME TO AN END FOR THE CORPS OF Discovery. It had now been more than 22 months since they had started their journey up the Missouri. The men paddling their rough dugouts and canoes against the current were long-haired, bearded, and probably none too clean. They were dressed from head to foot in elk skin. In appearance, little would have suggested that this was a detachment of the U.S. Army.

The men were happy to be heading home. They paddled 16 miles (25.7 km) upriver on March 23, their first day back on the Columbia, and another 16 the next day. A few days later they made 20 miles (32 km). That was an excellent rate of speed, considering they were now fighting the current. The weather was still disagreeably cold when they woke in the mornings, but signs of spring were all around.

A NEW RIVER AND A NEW MOUNTAIN

By the end of March, they were camped along the north side of the Columbia near the site of present-day Washougal, Washington. Their early departure from Fort Clatsop was now working to their disadvantage. On their first week on the river they bought dried fish from American Indians they met. However, the salmon had yet to make its annual appearance. Without a supply of fresh salmon, the American Indians had little food to spare.

Lewis and Clark halted for a week to restock their larder with venison and elk meat. On April 6, the Corps of Discovery resumed their trip. By mid-April, they reached the stretch of narrows, rapids, and falls east of the Cascades. They portaged their supplies on land. Some of the men pulled the empty canoes and dugouts upstream with towropes from the shore.

BAD MOOD ON THE COLUMBIA

The captains were eager to stop fighting the river currents. They wanted to strike off overland instead. For that they needed horses. Unfortunately the American Indians were not eager to sell them any. Clark spent several days in mid-April negotiating with American Indians. He

To the Umatilla and the Walla Walla, water was sacred and essential for the survival of all life. These people lived near the Columbia River and its tributaries and used it to fish, trade, and travel along using canoes. Tipis (teepees) were not traditionally used by the Umatilla (shown above, circa 1922); at the time of Lewis and Clark's visit, they lived in plank houses.

was able to purchase only a few broken-down mounts. By trading off their cooking kettles they acquired a few more horses. They had 10 in all. This was not nearly enough.

On April 21, the expedition set off on land along the north shore of the Columbia. A few of the men were assigned to paddle upriver in the two canoes. These carried gear that could not fit on their horses. The expedition eventually traded the remaining two canoes for some beads to increase their trade goods. They also managed to trade for a few more horses with American Indians they met along the way.

On April 27, they met up again with the Walla Walla chief Yellepit. Yellepit had welcomed then on their trip down the Columbia the previous fall. They spent several days with him and his tribe. The Indians brought them firewood and some fish. Lewis and Clark traded for additional horses. They were relieved to be back among friendly Indians. Yellepit presented Clark with a "very eligant white horse." Clark presented the chief with a sword, some gunpowder, and musket balls. Yellepit also told them of a "good road" with plenty of game that would cut 80 miles (128.7 km) from their return journey. It headed inland over territory that was new to them. Eventually, the road reconnected with the Snake River. With Yellepit's help they crossed the Columbia and left that river behind them for good.

BACK AMONG THE NEZ PERCE

The explorers reached the Snake River on May 4. They were now back among the Nez Perce. A few days later they met up with their old friend Chief Twisted Hair at a site near present-day Orofino, Idaho. The Nez Perce had kept their horses for them over the winter. They returned the 21 horses they were able to round up to the explorers. Lewis and Clark's men dug up the saddles and ammunition they had left in a cache by the Clearwater River.

At a council with Nez Perce chiefs, Lewis urged the Nez Perce to send a representative east to meet Thomas Jefferson. The Nez Perce were uninterested in making such a long journey eastward. They did, however, agree to send some young men with Lewis and Clark across the Bitterroot Mountains to talk peace with the Shoshone.

Just when they would be able to make that crossing of the mountains was a source of considerable concern to the captains. The Nez

Perce told Lewis and Clark that the winter snows had not yet melted. It would be another month before the Bitterroots were passable. This was unwelcome news. On May 14, they moved their camp a few miles eastward, to a site on the north bank of the Clearwater River near present-day Kamiah, Idaho. They would remain at this site from May 13 through June 9.

While they waited, they did what they could to stock up on food for crossing the Bitterroots. "[N]ot any of us," Lewis wrote, "have yet forgotten our sufferings in those mountains." The captains divided up the remaining stock of trade goods among the men. They traded with the Nez Perce for edible roots to add to their stock of rations. Lewis and Clark even cut the brass buttons from their coats to trade for more roots.

The Nez Perce seemed to genuinely like the explorers. Clark was valued as a healer. He treated dozens of Nez Perce for everything from sore eyes to paralysis. He seems to have cured some of his patients. He relieved others of the worst of their symptoms. Relations between the Nez Perce and the whites were also made stronger with dances, footraces, target-shooting contests, and other games.

BACK ACROSS THE BITTERROOTS

May turned to June. The Nez Perce still warned the captains that it was too soon to attempt the Bitterroots. They decided to press ahead on June 9. They spent several days hunting and preserving meat. On June 15, they headed up into the mountains.

They soon realized they should have listened to the Nez Perce. The horses floundered in the deep snow. There was no grass for them to eat. The expedition made it as far as Hungry Creek. The captains decided on June 17 that they would have to turn back. It was "the first time since we have been on this long tour," Lewis noted, "that we have ever been compelled to retreat . . ." Some of the men "were a good deel dejected."

On June 24, they set out again over the Bitterroots. This time they had the help of five Nez Perce men. They successfully crossed the mountains. Having expert guides made a big difference. Much of the snow had melted in the interval, revealing grass for the horses. On June 30, they finished crossing the mountains. It had taken them 11 days to cross the mountains heading west in fall 1805. In spring 1806, they completed the return trip in just six days.

DIVIDING THEIR FORCES

During the previous winter the captains decided to split up on the way home. Their plan was complicated. It depended a good deal on luck and timing. Lewis would lead a group eastward across the mountain pass that their Shoshone guide Old Toby had told them about the previous fall. This was supposed to be a shortcut back to the Great Falls of the Missouri. At the Great Falls, Lewis would divide his party again. He would take half of them on an overland route back to the Marias River. Lewis planned to see how far this river traveled toward the rich fur country of the Saskatchewan region.

Meanwhile, Clark was to lead the other half of the party. They would cross the Rockies by a new mountain pass. Their route would bring them back to the Three Forks of the Missouri. They believed this was a shorter route than the one they had followed across Lemhi Pass in summer 1805. At Three Forks, Clark would divide his own party. Half of his men would meet up with the group Lewis left at the Great Falls. Clark would proceed overland to the Yellowstone River. He would follow it back to its mouth on the Missouri. The men at Great Falls would continue down the Missouri. They would meet up with Lewis. This group would journey to the mouth of the Yellowstone. There, Lewis and Clark and the entire Corps of Discovery would reunite.

Lewis and Clark said good-bye to each other on the morning of July 3. "I took leave of my worthy friend and companion, Capt. Clark," Lewis wrote in his journal that evening. "I could not avoid feeling much concern on this occasion although I hoped this seperation was only momentary."

Lewis and nine of the men rode north along the Bitterroot River. The five Nez Perce men went with them and left the group on July 4. The pass over which Lewis and his men crossed the Continental Divide is now known as Lewis and Clark Pass. On July 11, they reached the site of one of their former camps on the Missouri. The trip overland had taken them just eight days. They killed a buffalo that day. It was their first taste of their favorite meat since the previous summer. Less happily, thieves made off with 10 of their 17 horses that night.

Meanwhile, Clark's party followed a separate route back to the Missouri. They, too, made rapid progress. On July 4, 1806, they celebrated their third Independence Day on the trail. On July 6, they crossed the Continental Divide. The mountain pass they used is now known as Gibbons Pass. Two days later they reached the place where Sacagawea had reunited with her brother, Cameahwait, the previous year. Clark and his men reached the Three Forks of the Missouri on July 13.

EXPLORING THE YELLOWSTONE RIVER

At the Three Forks, Clark's party split. Ten men headed back down the Missouri to the Great Falls. Clark and 12 others, including Charbonneau, Sacagawea, and little Pomp, set out on horseback to the Yellowstone. "The Indian woman . . . has been of great service to me as a pilot through this Country," Clark noted in his journal. Sacagawea had just helped guide the group through a mountain pass that she thought was the best route to the Yellowstone valley. It is known today as Bozeman Pass. On July 19, they made camp along the Yellowstone.

Clark's party reached the junction of the Yellowstone and Missouri rivers on August 3. They were supposed to wait there to meet up with Lewis's party coming down the Missouri. However, Clark decided to move his camp farther east along the Missouri. He left a note for Lewis attached to a discarded elk antler.

LEWIS'S ENCOUNTER WITH THE BLACKFEET

Lewis, meanwhile, divided his party back at Great Falls. He left Sergeant Gass and five men there to wait for the 10 men from Clark's party. From Great Falls the group would portage the expedition's supplies, including the precious journals, around the falls. Then they would recover the white pirogue for the return trip to St. Louis.

On July 16, Lewis, Drouillard, and Joseph and Reubin Field headed off on horseback. They followed the northern edge of the Missouri. Then they turned northward, along the the Marias River. Lewis knew this was a risky trip. The region around the Marias River was home to the Blackfeet, who bullied the Shoshone and Nez Perce tribes. The Blackfeet traded their furs with the British in Canada. As a result, they were well armed. They were unlikely to look kindly on the coming of traders from the United States who might supply their enemies with similar weapons.

Lewis and his party kept a sharp lookout for the Blackfeet as they headed upriver. On July 21, they came to a fork in the river. They chose to follow the more northerly fork, Cut Bank Creek; however, the river bent westward. Arriving at "a clump of large cottonwood trees" the next day, Lewis halted his party. He could see that the river rose into the mountains, northeast of present-day Browning, Montana. They camped that night at what Lewis named Camp Disappointment. He admitted to himself that the headwaters of the Marias "will not be as far north as I wished and expected."

Lewis and his men stayed at Camp Disappointment for several days. Lewis wanted to fix the location's longitude and latitude. For this, he had to wait for clear skies. On July 25, the men discovered signs of a recently abandoned Indian camp. Lewis wrote, "[W]e consider ourselves extreemly fortunate in not having met with these people." Their luck was about to take a turn for the worse.

The following day, Lewis and his men were finally heading back to the Missouri. They encountered "a very unpleasant sight." They came across eight Blackfeet caring for a herd of about 30 horses. Lewis "resolved to make the best of our situation and to approach them in a friendly manner." He had his men ride up to the Blackfeet on horseback, flying the American flag. Lewis handed out a handkerchief, a flag, and a medal to three of the young men. Using sign language to communicate, Lewis invited the Blackfeet to camp with them.

Once settled in camp, Lewis explained how he had traveled all the way "to the great waters where the sun sets." Along the way, he "had seen a great many nations, all of whom I had invited to come and trade with me on the rivers on this side of the mountain . . ." The men smoked a pipe together. Lewis invited the Blackfeet to accompany him down to the Missouri.

Trouble came at first light the next day. Joseph Field was on sentry duty. He was supposed to alert Lewis and the others if there was trouble. He got careless and laid his rifle down on the ground. One of the Blackfeet jumped up and seized both Joseph and Reubin Field's rifles and ran off. Joseph woke up his brother and the two set out after him in hot pursuit. Reubin, who had picked up his knife, stabbed the thief to death.

Lewis and Drouillard woke up. Other Blackfeet were trying to steal their rifles. Drouillard wrestled his gun back. Lewis shouted and drew

Once the Blackfeet learned from Lewis that the Nez Perce and Shoshone, their mortal enemies, would be receiving guns and supplies in a deal with the U.S. government, the tribe saw the Americans as a threat to Blackfeet power. In this etching by Patrick Gass, Captain Lewis is shown in the only fight that took place on the entire expedition. After an attempt by the Blackfeet to steal the expedition's guns, Lewis raised his gun and shot one of them.

his pistol on the man who had his rifle. The man threw it on the ground. Then other Blackfeet tried to drive off the whites' horses. Lewis pursued two of them. One of them stopped and hid behind some rocks. The other turned, musket in his hand. Lewis got off the first shot, killing the native. However, before he died he shot at Lewis, who "felt the wind of his bullet very distinctly." The other native was still hidden nearby, armed with a bow and arrow. Lewis made a quick return to camp.

Two of the Blackfeet were now dead or dying. The other six were still capable of fighting. They might even find other Blackfeet to join them to seek revenge. Lewis, Drouillard, and the Field brothers hurriedly gathered up their supplies. They burned the Indians' shields and weapons. Lewis hung the peace medal he had given the Blackfeet around the neck of one of the dead men. He did this "that they might be informed who we were." This was not quite what the medals had been intended for.

They galloped off across the plains. After covering nearly 100 miles (160 km) they stopped at 2:00 A.M. on July 28. At first light, Lewis and the men rode again. They reached the Missouri at midafternoon. There they found 15 well-armed men of the Corps of Discovery heading down the river. The explorers arrived at the mouth of the Marias. They dug up the supplies they had left there on the way west. They had hoped to refloat the red pirogue, but it was badly rotted. The white pirogue was now the last remnant of the fleet that began the Corps of Discovery's journey up the Missouri.

BACK ON THE MISSOURI

On August 7, Lewis and his men reached the junction of the Missouri and Yellowstone rivers. It was a great disappointment that Clark was not there to meet them. They found Clark's note still attached to the elk antler. They were eager to reunite the expedition, so they kept moving. Before they found Clark, Lewis had another brush with death. On August 11, Lewis and Cruzatte were hunting. Lewis's one-eyed companion mistook him for an elk and shot him in the buttocks. The wound was painful but not fatal. Lewis traveled most of the rest of the way down the Missouri lying on his stomach while his buttocks healed.

The next day they met up with two white men, Joseph Dickson and Forest Hancock. These were the first whites that they had seen since departing the Mandan village in April 1805. The men from Illinois had spent two years hunting, trapping, and trading with the American Indians. Dickson and Hancock told Lewis that they had met Clark the previous day. Soon Lewis and his party caught up with Clark's group. Their meeting place on the Missouri is known as "Reunion Point." It is six miles (9.6 km) south of present-day Sanish, North Dakota. The Corps of Discovery, after many misadventures, was united and on its way home.

On August 14, they reached the Mandan villages. There they said good-bye to Charbonneau, Sacagawea, and Pomp. Clark paid Charbonneau $500. In his own mind, Clark may have thought Sacagawea deserved the money more. A few days later he wrote a letter to Charbonneau. "Your woman," he wrote, "who accompanied you that long dangerous and fatigueing rout to the Pacific Ocian and back diserved a greater reward for her attention and services on that rout than we had in our power to give her."

On August 17, Lewis and Clark proceeded down the Missouri. The Corps of Discovery had some additional companions. The Mandan chief Sheheke and his family came with them. They planned to travel to Washington to meet the new Great White Father.

As they continued down the river, they saw more familiar faces. These included the Arikara and the Yankton Nakota. On September 4, they stopped to pay their respects to Sergeant Floyd where they had left him buried on a hillside overlooking the Missouri. The familiar sights of the lower Missouri passed by rapidly. They traveled up to 50 miles (80 km) a day. This was better than three times their average mileage heading up the river in 1804. Unlike their earlier trip, they now found the Missouri crowded with other travelers. Before they reached the river's mouth they met nearly 150 traders and trappers heading up the river. The Missouri was becoming a great highway into the Louisiana Territory. This was just as Jefferson had foreseen. They picked up news from the travelers. They also happily stocked up on supplies. Lewis's wound was healing. By September 9, Clark reported him all but fully recovered.

On September 20, they saw cows on the shoreline. This was "a joy-full Sight to the party . . ." Clark noted. It meant they had reached the edge of white settlement. In the late afternoon on September 21, they arrived in St. Charles, Missouri. The town's inhabitants cheered, fed, and sheltered the explorers they had last seen in May 1804. On September 22, they traveled on to the newly established Fort Bellefontaine. This was the first permanent U.S. Army post west of the Mississippi. Their brother officers saluted them by firing from the fort's guns.

The great moment of triumph came the next day, September 23. They proceeded down the Missouri to its very end. They made a quick visit to their old camp across the Mississippi. Then they sailed back across the river to St. Louis, Missouri. The city's inhabitants lined the shore. They gave three cheers as the Corps of Discovery came into view. The men clambered out of the white pirogue and the canoes. According to Sergeant Ordway, writing his last journal entry that day, the men "rejoiced" to find themselves safe and well at the end of the expedition. "[W]e entend to return to our native homes to See our parents once more as we have been So long from them."

It had been two years, four months, and 10 days since the Corps of Discovery set off in search of the Northwest Passage. They had explored roughly 8,000 miles (12,874 km) of territory. Lewis announced their success in a letter to President Jefferson on September 23: "It is with pleasure that I anounce to you the safe arrival of myself and party at 12 Oclk. today. . . . In obedience to your orders we have penitrated the Continent of North America to the Pacific Ocean. . . .”

THE LIVES OF LEWIS AND CLARK

At first, Lewis and Clark enjoyed newfound celebrity and its rewards. There were public celebrations, balls, and tributes in their honor. Important men wanted to shake their hands. Congress voted to offer Lewis $3,600 in back pay. This was a lot of money in those days. He was given 1,600 acres of western land. Jefferson appointed Lewis governor of the Upper Louisiana Territory. This job gave him a steady salary and the chance to become an investor in the profitable fur-trade that would soon take over the West. Clark reaped similar financial rewards. He was made the superintendent of Indian affairs for the Louisiana Territory and brigadier general of militia for the territory. In spring 1807, it seemed that both men, still in their thirties and in excellent health, enjoyed the prospect of long, honorable, and prosperous lives and careers stretching before them.

In 1813, William Clark became the first governor of the Missouri Territory. In 1808, he married Julia Hancock, the young woman also known as Judith for whom he named Judith’s River in Montana. It was a happy marriage, and they had five children. Clark and his wife adopted Sacagawea’s son Jean Baptiste—“Pomp”—and raised him as their own. Clark died in 1838 and was buried in St. Louis’s Bellefontaine Cemetery. The monument above his grave bears the inscription “His life is written in the History of His Country.”

For Meriwether Lewis, things did not work out as happily. He proved an inept and unpopular governor. He was unlucky in both love and business. En route to Washington in fall 1809, he was overcome by depression. On the night of October 11, Lewis took his own life while staying at a roadhouse in Grinder’s Stand, Tennessee. William Clark and Thomas Jefferson were grief-stricken to learn of Lewis’s fate. However, neither man was surprised. “I fear O! I fear the weight of his mind has overcome him,” Clark wrote on hearing the sad news. Lewis was buried near the site of his death. The papers he carried with him, including the original field journals and maps of the Lewis and Clark expedition, were returned to Clark.

THE FATES OF THE CORPS OF DISCOVERY

The members of the Corps of Discovery lived out the rest of their lives in different ways. Several expedition members died violently. George Drouillard and John Potts were killed by Lewis's old foes, the Blackfeet. John Colter almost shared their fate. He was captured by the Blackfeet, but they decided to give Colter a sporting chance before killing him. They took all his clothes and let him run for his life. Incredibly, his feet torn and bloody, he managed to outrun his pursuers. He died a peaceful death in Missouri in 1813. George Shannon was another expedition member who had a close encounter with death. He was shot in the leg in a hostile encounter with the Arikara Indians in 1807. His leg was amputated, but he survived to become a lawyer and lived on to 1836. Sergeant Patrick Gass outlived everyone from the expedition. He fought in the War of 1812, married at age 60, fathered six children, and died at age 98.

William Clark freed York about 10 years after the expedition. York became a firefighter and died of cholera. Sacagawea is the most famous member of the Lewis and Clark expedition after the captains themselves. There are widely varying accounts of her later life. Some believe that she moved back to the Rockies and lived to old age, dying in 1884. The more likely account suggests that she died in December 1812 at Fort Manuel, a fur-trading post on the upper Missouri, shortly after bearing her second child. An American fur trader reported her death to Clark. He wrote that she was "the best woman in the Fort."

THE WEST SINCE LEWIS AND CLARK'S DAY

Much has changed in the American landscape since Lewis and Clark's day. Interstate highways replace dusty or muddy tracks on the land. The rivers have changed too. As Lewis's biographer Stephen Ambrose wrote, "Today, Lewis and Clark would hardly recognize much of the Missouri River. The river is 127 miles shorter, one-third as wide, and far deeper

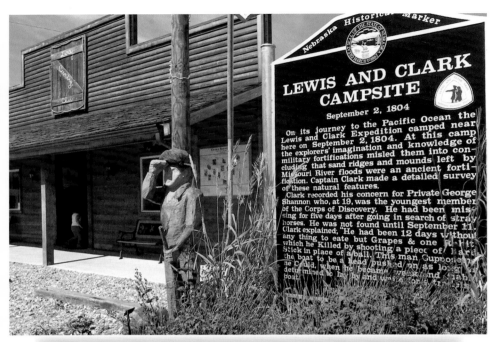

At a campsite in Lindy, Nebraska, stands a statue of Private George Shannon next to a plaque commemorating the Lewis and Clark expedition. Shannon nearly died of starvation when he got lost for 16 days in present-day northeast Nebraska. Today, visitors can visit more than 100 sites along the Lewis and Clark National Historic Trail, including the 240-mile (386-km) Shannon Trail, named after George Shannon.

and faster." The Missouri has been transformed for much of its length by dams, levees, and reservoirs. The Great Falls of the Missouri is no longer very great. It is mostly covered by water backed up from the Ryan Dam. Many of Lewis and Clark's campsites in eastern Montana now lie beneath the waters of the Fort Peck Reservoir. The site of Camp Fortunate now lies under the waters of the Clark Canyon Reservoir. There are also four dams along the stretch of the Columbia River explored by Lewis and Clark. They have tamed and drowned the falls and rapids that caused the explorers so much trouble. They have also severely curtailed the salmon run on the river.

The words of the Lewis and Clark expedition live on. Lewis and Clark's journals were contained in 18 red leatherbound notebooks. They were deposited in the archives of the American Philosophical Society in

Philadelphia. For nearly a century they were forgotten. In 1904, on the expedition's centennial, a complete edition of the original journals was published. In the years that followed, other documents from the expedition turned up at irregular intervals. Sergeant Ordway's journal was not found until 1916. Some of Clark's field notes turned up only in 1953.

THE LEGACY OF LEWIS AND CLARK

Their names survive, their words survive, and so do their contributions in exploration and discovery. Lewis and Clark did not find the Northwest Passage. They accomplished something greater. Americans would have found their path to the Pacific in time. In fact, they would soon find shorter and better routes to the Pacific. What made Lewis and Clark true pathfinders was the impact they had on the American imagination. The journey of the Corps of Discovery established the destiny of the United States as a continental power. It was a nation that stretched from sea to sea. The *West,* that place that existed as a blank spot on the map prior to 1804, became in the nation's imagination the *American West* after 1806. People could go there and come back. It had been done. It could be done again.

Chronology

1801   Thomas Jefferson becomes president of the United States.

◆ Meriwether Lewis becomes Jefferson's personal secretary; lives in East Room of the White House. With Jefferson's support, Lewis plans expedition to explore the West.

1803   *Spring:* Lewis sent to Philadelphia to study botany, zoology, celestial navigation, and medicine from nation's leading scientists. Begins buying supplies for expedition.

Timeline

1803
William Clark becomes co-commander of the Corps of Discovery

1804
MARCH 14 Corps of Discovery sets off on expedition from Camp Dubois

AUGUST 3 First official council between representatives of the United States and Western Indians occurs between Corps and Missouri and Oto Indians

1803

1805

1803
SUMMER Jefferson more than doubles the size of the United States for $15 million with the Louisiana Purchase

1804
AUGUST 20 Sergeant Floyd dies, first casualty of expedition

NOVEMBER 4 Sacagawea becomes interpreter on expedition

1805
LATE JULY Expedition reaches Three Forks of the Missouri, names the Gallatin, Madison, and Jefferson

- William Clark accepts Lewis's invitation to share command of the expedition, called Corps of Discovery.

- *Summer:* Jefferson more than doubles the size of the United States for $15 million with the Louisiana Purchase.

- Lewis oversees construction of keelboat in Pittsburgh, then sails down the Ohio River to pick up Clark and recruits along the way.

- *Fall/Winter:* Camp Wood (also called Camp Dubois) is established on east bank of Mississippi, upstream from St. Louis. More men recruited.

1804   *March 10:* Lewis and Clark attend ceremonies in St. Louis handing over Louisiana Territory from France to the United States.

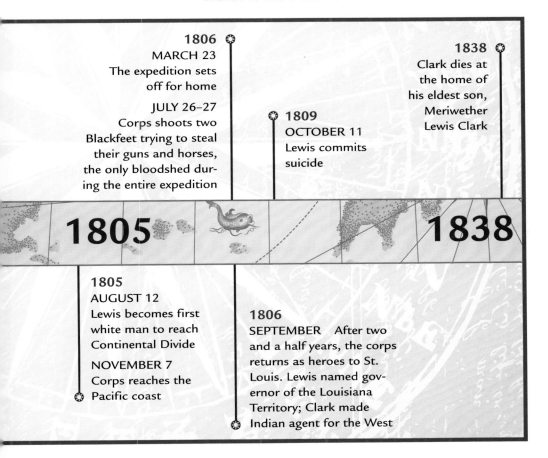

1806
MARCH 23
The expedition sets off for home

JULY 26–27
Corps shoots two Blackfeet trying to steal their guns and horses, the only bloodshed during the entire expedition

1809
OCTOBER 11
Lewis commits suicide

1838
Clark dies at the home of his eldest son, Meriwether Lewis Clark

1805

1838

1805
AUGUST 12
Lewis becomes first white man to reach Continental Divide

NOVEMBER 7
Corps reaches the Pacific coast

1806
SEPTEMBER   After two and a half years, the corps returns as heroes to St. Louis. Lewis named governor of the Louisiana Territory; Clark made Indian agent for the West

- *March 14:* Corps of Discovery, nearly four dozen men, sets off from Camp Dubois.

- *May 25:* Expedition passes La Charette, the last settlement of whites.

- *August 3:* First official council between representatives of the United States and Western Indians occurs when members of Corps of Discovery meet with delegation of Missouri and Oto Indians.

- *August 20:* Sergeant Charles Floyd becomes first casualty of the expedition when he dies of what is now thought of as a burst appendix. Men name hilltop where he is buried Floyd's Bluff.

- *September 7:* Now in the Great Plains, expedition sees animals unknown in the East: coyote, antelope, deer. In total, the captains record in their journals 178 plants and 122 animals.

- *November 4:* Captains hire Toussaint Charbonneau and his Shoshone wife, Sacagawea, to help them find the Shoshones that they have been told live at the headwaters of the Missouri and have many horses.

- *December 17:* The expedition move into Fort Mandan for the winter.

1805 *February 11:* Sacagawea gives birth to her son, Jean Baptiste.

- *April 7:* About a dozen men from the corps sail back downriver, along with maps, reports, Indian artifacts, and boxes of scientific specimens for President Jefferson.

- *April 29:* Lewis and another hunter kill a grizzly bear, which has never been seen before by science.

- *May 3:* The corps enters the White Cliffs of the Missouri, sandstone formations the men compare to the ruins of an ancient city. This section is now one of the most unspoiled sections of the Lewis and Clark route and is protected by Congress.

- *Late July:* Expedition reaches Three Forks of the Missouri, which the captains name the Gallatin (after Secretary of Treasury Albert Gallatin), the Jefferson (after Thomas Jefferson), and the Madison (after Secretary of States James Madison).

- *August 12:* Lewis becomes first white man to reach the Continental Divide.

- *August 17:* Clark arrives and Sacagawea is brought in to translate. The Shoshone chief, Cameawhaite, turns out to be her brother.

- *September 11:* The corps is on the brink of starvation, and they must slaughter a horse for food. Eleven days later they stagger out of the Bitterroot Mountains, which Patrick Gass calls "the most terrible mountains I have ever beheld."

- *October 16:* The men reach the Columbia River.

- *November 7:* The corps reaches the Pacific coast. After taking a vote (including York, the slave, and Indian woman Sacagawea), they decide to build winter quarters in present-day Astoria, Oregon.

1806 *March 23:* The expedition sets off for home.

- *July 3:* The corps splits into smaller groups in order to explore the Louisiana Territory. Clarks takes a group down the Yellowstone River; Lewis takes a group across a shortcut to the Great Falls and the Marias River.

- *July 26-27:* Lewis catches some men from the Blackfeet tribe trying to steal their horses and guns, a fight breaks out. Two Blackfeet are killed, the only bloodshed during the entire expedition.

- *August:* The men reunite with Clark and the rest of the corps on August 12.

- They arrive back at the Mandan villages and say good-bye to Sacagawea, Charbonneau, and Jean Baptiste.

- *September:* After two and a half years, the corps makes it back to St. Louis. The men are national heroes. Balls and galas are held in towns they pass through in their honor. Lewis is named governor of the Louisiana Territory; Clark is made Indian agent for the West and brigadier general of the territory's militia.

1809   *October 11:* Lewis commits suicide at an inn south of Nashville, Tennessee.

1812   Sacagawea dies in South Dakota, and Clark assumes custody of Jean Baptiste and her infant daughter, Lisette.

1832   York, Clark's slave, dies of cholera after having worked in the freighting business in Tennessee and Kentucky. Clark had kept him as a slave for 10 years after the expedition before granting him his freedom.

1838   Clark dies at the home of his eldest son, Meriwether Lewis Clark.

Glossary

bilious—A medical condition thought to do with a malfunction of the liver, or the production of excess bile; a term also associated in the early nineteenth century with malaria.

botany—The branch of biology that deals with plant life.

cache—A hiding place in the ground for provisions.

cartography—The design and production of maps.

chronometer—An especially accurate timekeeper used to determine longitude.

colic—A pain in the stomach or bowels.

confluence—A flowing together of two or more streams or rivers.

continental divide—High ground dividing river systems that flow into different oceans.

dram—A small drink of liquor.

dysentery—An infectious stomach illness.

espontoon (spontoon)—An eighteenth-century infantry officer's weapon; a spear-headed brace that could be used to steady a rifle for more accurate firing. Lewis and Clark used theirs as a walking stick, rifle rest, and weapon.

estuary—The part of the mouth of a river emptying into the ocean in which the river's flow is affected by the ocean's tides.

ethnography—The scientific description and study of various human cultures and races.

headwaters—The origin of a stream or river.

keelboat—A shallow freight boat used for river travel.

latitude—The angular distance north or south from the equator of a point on Earth's surface, measured on the meridian of the point.

longitude—The angular distance east or west on Earth's surface, determined by the angle contained between the meridian of a particular place and the prime meridian in Greenwich, England.

meridian—A great circle of Earth passing through the poles and any given point on Earth's surface.

naturalist—Someone engaged in the study of natural history, such as zoology and botany.

paleontology—The study of forms of life existing in former geological periods, as represented by fossil remains.

pirogue—A small wooden watercraft. *Pirogue* is a French word that in the Canadian fur trade was used to describe a large dugout canoe. Lewis and Clark's "pirogues," however, seem to have been more on the order of a large, open lifeboat, flat-bottomed, with plank sides, and carrying a mast.

portage—The act of carrying boats or goods from one navigable body of water to another, or the place where such things can be carried.

sovereignty—The supreme and independent authority of government to which others are subordinate.

tributary—A stream contributing its flow to a larger stream or body of water.

watershed—A high point of land dividing two river drainage areas.

zoology—The branch of the biological sciences that concerns the study of animals.

Bibliography

Ambrose, Stephen E. *Undaunted Courage: Meriwether Lewis, Thomas Jefferson, and the Opening of the American West.* New York: Simon and Schuster, 1996.

Botkin, Daniel B. *Our Natural History: The Lessons of Lewis and Clark.* New York: G.P. Putnam's Sons, 1995.

Calloway, Colin G. *One Vast Winter Count: The Native American West Before Lewis and Clark.* Lincoln: University of Nebraska Press, 2003.

Dramer, Kim. *The Shoshone.* Philadelphia: Chelsea House Publishers, 1996.

Duncan, Dayton. *Out West: A Journey Through Lewis and Clark's America.* 2nd ed. Lincoln: University of Nebraska Press, 2000.

Furtwangler, Albert. *Acts of Discovery: Visions of America in the Lewis and Clark Journals.* Urbana: University of Illinois Press, 1993.

Kessler, Donna J. *The Making of Sacagawea: A Euro-American Legend.* Tuscaloosa: University of Alabama Press, 1996.

Kroll, Steven. *Lewis and Clark: Explorers of the American West.* New York: Holiday House, 1994.

McMurtry, Larry. *Sacagawea's Nickname: Essays on the American West.* New York: New York Review Books, 2001.

Moulton, Gary E, ed. *The Journals of the Lewis and Clark Expedition.* 13 vols. Lincoln: University of Nebraska Press, 1983–1999.

———. *The Lewis and Clark Journals: An American Epic of Discovery.* Lincoln: University of Nebraska Press, 2003.

Ronda, James P. *Jefferson's West: A Journey with Lewis and Clark.* Monticello, Va.: Thomas Jefferson Foundation, 2000.

Schwantee, Carlos, ed. *Encounters with a Distant Land: Exploration and the Great Northwest.* Moscow: University of Idaho Press, 1994.

Wilson, James. *The Earth Shall Weep: A History of Native America.* New York: Atlantic Monthly Press, 1999.

Woodger, Elin, and Brandon Toropor. *Encyclopedia of the Lewis and Clark Expedition.* New York: Facts On File, 2004.

Further Resources

Glancy, Diane. *Stone Heart: A Novel of Sacajawea.* New York: Overlook Press, 2003.

Hall, Brian. *I Should Be Extremely Happy in Your Company: A Novel of Lewis and Clark.* New York: Viking Press, 2003.

Lasky, Kathryn. *The Journal of Augustus Pelletier: The Lewis and Clark Expedition, 1804 (My Name Is America).* New York: Scholastic, 2000.

Myers, Laurie. *Lewis and Clark and Me: A Dog's Tale.* New York: Henry Holt and Co., 2002.

Thom, James Alexander. *Sign-Talker: The Adventure of George Drouillard on the Lewis and Clark Expedition.* New York: Ballantine Books, 2001.

Roop, Connie, and Peter Roop. *Girl of the Shining Mountains: Sacagawea's Story.* New York: Hyperion Press, 1999.

WEB SITES

Discovering Lewis and Clark
http://www.lewis-clark.org/
Sponsored by the Lewis and Clark Fort Mandan Foundation, this site has interactive features, journal entries, biographies, and information about regional Native American tribes.

Go West Across America with Lewis and Clark
http://www.nationalgeographic.com/west
This interactive Web site for students provides information and enhances online learning opportunities

Lewis and Clark: Mapping the West
http://www.edgate.com/lewisandclark
Sponsored by the Smithsonian National Museum of Natural History, this site has photographs, maps, teacher-designed lesson plans, and other primary resources.

Lewis and Clark National Historic Trail
http://www.nps.gov/lecl
The National Park Service's site for information about the Lewis and Clark National Historic Trail. Includes photographs, biographies, and information for kids.

Lewis and Clark Trail Heritage Foundation
http://www.lewisandclark.org/
This foundation, which has 36 chapters, focuses on preserving the Lewis and Clark Trail and its stories.

Picture Credits

Index

About the Contributors

Author and general editor **MAURICE ISSERMAN** holds a B.A. in history from Reed College and an M.A. and Ph.D. in history from the University of Rochester. He is a professor of history at Hamilton College, specializing in twentieth-century U.S. history and the history of exploration. Isserman was a Fulbright distinguished lecturer at Moscow State University. He is the author of 12 books.

General editor **JOHN S. BOWMAN** received a B.A. in English literature from Harvard University and matriculated at Trinity College, Cambridge University, as Harvard's Fiske Scholar and at the University of Munich. Bowman has worked as an editor and as a freelance writer for more than 40 years. He has edited numerous works of history, as well as served as general editor of Chelsea House's AMERICA AT WAR set. Bowman is the author of more than 10 books, including a volume in this series, *Exploration in the World of the Ancients, Revised Edition*.